DID YOU ME CRYING

The moving story of survival through 45 years of sexual, physical and emotional abuse

lip

Cassie Moore

First published in 2012 by:

Live It Publishing
27 Old Gloucester Road
London, United Kingdom.
WC1N 3AX
www.liveitpublishing.com

Copyright © 2012 by Cassie Moore

The moral right of Cassie Moore to be identified as the author of this work has been asserted by her in accordance with the Copyright, Designs and Patents Act 1988.

All rights reserved.

Except as permitted under current legislation, no part of this work may be photocopied, stored in a retrieval system, published, performed in public, adapted, broadcast, transmitted, recorded or reproduced in any form or by any means, without the prior permission of the copyright owners.

This is a work of non-fiction. The events and experiences detailed herein have been faithfully rendered as the author has remembered them, to the best of her ability. The names and identifying characteristics of numerous individuals have been changed throughout this book in order to protect their anonymity and privacy.

All enquiries should be addressed to Live It Publishing.

ISBN 978-1-906954-59-8 (pbk)

Contents

1. Beginnings 3
2. Responsibilities 23
3. On The Outside Looking In 40
4. 'Mammy, I'm Bleeding' 45
5. A Schoolgirl Crush 54
6. Married Life 67
7. Allegations 76
8. My Knight in Shining Armour 84
9. Doubts 95
10. A Second Marriage 105
11. The Fight for Stephanie, and a New Baby 117
12. Confrontations 125
13. An Unexpected Pregnancy 133
14. Slipping 144
15. Life Alone 150
16. Back to Ireland 160
17. Fighting Back 177
18. Finally Free 192
Epilogue 196

I was but a child when you took my innocence away. What was going through your sick mind as you repeatedly raped me? When I pleaded with you, 'please Daddy, no!' How could you smile at me when you could see pure fear in my little eyes? How could you get pleasure from a child so small, so young, so vulnerable? Do you remember I cried in pain with every thrust, as you strived to gain your sick gratification? Do you remember how you stank of diesel and body odour, and how your disgusting heavy frame loomed over my tiny body and hurt me so badly? Do you remember my little legs barely able to stand as the fear and pain you caused in me almost made my knees buckle? Did you ever look in my eyes and feel disgust for what you were doing? Do you remember you would throw me around like a little rag doll and make me believe that it was all my fault? Did you hear me crying?

Chapter 1

Beginnings

I was born in July 1966 in Dublin city. My mother was 19 years old when I was born: she was unmarried when I was conceived, such a shameful thing in 1960s Ireland. Two months before I was born she married the man I thought was my father, but I was later to find out he was my stepfather. He was 17 years old.

My mother was quite small with long flowing dark hair. She didn't have many teeth, but her top teeth were very prominent and stuck out over her bottom lip. She was a cold, self-absorbed woman, who suffered from depression. She spent a lot of my childhood in and out of hospital having electric shock therapy, or other treatments to try and help her with the depression. She would always come home from hospital with an array of tablets of all different shapes and colours. My mother also had a very vicious temper which she used to unleash on me, but I still loved her dearly.

My stepfather on the other hand, although overweight was a handsome man – tall, with slicked-back hair like a teddy boy and a beard. He was a magnet for other women, and made use of the opportunities this presented, which added to my mother's pain greatly. He worked in construction, and was loved and adored by all for his seemingly devilish charm, but he too had a vicious temper which my mother and I were on the receiving end of many times. He was a domineering, terrifying man. To say I loved him would be a lie – I feared him and very early on began to really dislike him.

I remember my mother's delight in telling me that my stepfather in one of his many tempers, held me over some banisters when I was 6 weeks old and threatened to drop me. I was reminded from a very young age, that my very existence was the cause of everything that was wrong in the world, that I was definitely a mistake and should never have been born. I became used to hearing this over the years, but I never stopped hurting at hearing those horrid words.

My life began in Glasnevin, north Dublin, but my first real memory is when I was three years old and we were living in Ballymun. By this time my mother had two more little girls. Sharon was 11 months younger than me and Patricia was born the following year.

Like many families at that time we were very poor. We didn't have proper beds, we slept on the floor with old coats over us for warmth. Food was in very short supply. We didn't have much furniture, just a rickety old table, two delapidated chairs and a black and white TV.

I remember my mother and stepfather were always fighting, my mother crying, he shouting. We children were frightened, hungry and unloved. Things were so bad, the year I turned three years old, my mother placed me in a children's home. She took great delight in telling me how neglected I was when she decided to come and get me, and how grateful I should be that she did come. She told me she didn't recognise me at all until I called out to her. My face was covered in cold sores, all that was

CHAPTER 1: BEGINNINGS

showing were my two eyes. I had rickets, jaundice and hepatitis. I was taken straight to hospital where I remember being in a cot, nurses and doctors smiling at me, calling me by a film star's name. I remember being confused as to why they called me that. Many years later I smiled when I realised who they meant. I have never forgotten that time. Looking back I guess it was unusual to have anyone pay any positive attention to me at that time.

But it wasn't long until I was back in our bare flat in Ballymun, back to the screaming and shouting, back to the battering, back to the abuse.

I remember in those days my stepfather would go to a pub that was frequented by many of the men from Ballymun. He was not a big drinker really, so I cannot put his violence or abuse down to drinking. I can only say it was pure, sober evil. My mother would go and play bingo, as many mothers from Ballymun would. The difference was most other mums and dads would organise a baby-sitter, but we didn't have anything like that. They would put me and my two sisters to bed, then go out and leave us. I remember I woke up many times to an empty flat. I would wander around the flat and cry for my mother until she came home. She would smack me hard for being out of bed, drag me by the arm with my little legs dangling, as she threw me back to my makeshift bed on the floor. No hug, no kiss, no comfort.

One night they were out I got very distressed. I remember dragging a chair from the kitchen into the hallway, and standing on it to open the front door so I could go and look for them. I remember standing on the balcony, very cold and frightened, no shoes on, just a vest. It was so dark, I started crying, until one of the neighbours came out and found me. She picked me up in her arms and brought me back inside our flat and stayed with me until my mother came home.

When my mother finally did come home she was so mad with me for being up yet again and for leaving my sisters. She said I was such a bad girl, shouting at me that I was nothing but trouble to her and a big mistake. She slapped me so hard for that. My little escapade put paid to her nights out and boy was she mad!

The day came for me to start school. I remember I didn't feel any excitement or any nerves. I had already developed the knack of detaching myself from situations, almost like I was looking in but not part of what was going on. I looked around the classroom and saw other children crying and being hugged by their mothers, but I still didn't feel anything. I was neither pleased or displeased to be there, nor was I frightened, nor was I upset. As I watched this display of open affection and emotion I looked around for my mother, only to see her disappear out of the door. There were no hugs for me, no, 'have a good day darling', not that I was bothered by her disappearance, and if she had done any of those things I think I wouldn't have known how to react.

I found school quite difficult in all areas, academically and socially. I was a dreamer: if I didn't understand things I would switch off; if I was being told off I would switch off; if I was being teased and bullied I would switch off. I spent most of my school days feeling detached from those around me. At a young age I had developed a stammer, my mother had hit me very hard on the head over something and that's when the stammer started. It particularly affected me when I was asked to stand up

CHAPTER 1: BEGINNINGS

in class and read. One teacher in particular would constantly pick on me to get up and read aloud, and of course I would stutter and stammer my way through it, much to her amusement. This would cause me such distress that I would wet myself. She would encourage the class to mimic me, but, I would escape by switching off and going into my dreamworld quite easily.

My mother didn't collect me from school very often – even from a very early age I would make my own way home. I remember I would saunter up the road singing. I always loved to sing, lost in a beautiful dreamworld. I would sing 'Nobody's Child', a song my mother said was especially for me.

The black and white television would go to the pawnshop every now and again, but when we did have it I would love to watch *Bagpuss*. I thought it was the best thing in the whole world. I would have given anything to have been Emily. One morning when I was about four years old I came into the kitchen to find my mother in a haze of cigarette smoke crying once again, the flat looked emptier than usual, she told me we had been robbed, and they had taken the few things we had. My beloved television was gone, no more *Bagpuss*.

My mother and stepfather continued to fight, only the fights got more violent. My mother became more and more upset and our flat was a war zone. She found out that my stepfather was having an affair with some blonde beauty on the estate. Things were really bad, and about to get worse for me.

I have been asked several times, when the abuse first started, and I have to be honest, I don't ever remember not being abused. But an incident that happened when I was four, was to be the start of a nightmare that I was to endure for all of my childhood years and was to be the pattern of things to come for me, for many more years after that.

One Saturday afternoon my mother went out, I guess to do some shopping or the like. She took my sister Sharon with her, my stepfather was looking after me and my younger sister Patricia who was still a baby in her pram. We had somehow managed to get another TV, I remember the horse racing was on. My stepfather was sitting on the sofa – he never really spoke gently to me, preferring to shout and frighten the life out of me, but this day was different, he spoke very softly and smiled at me. He told me to come and sit with him, he put my hand on his crotch and said 'Daddy wants you to play.' Delighted that I was getting some attention I was only too pleased to play. I was only four years old. I didn't understand what was happening and willingly went along with what he wanted because he was being so nice to me. He took out his penis and told me it was a lily. He told me to rub it and showed me how. I didn't at that time think anything was wrong, so I did what he asked.

After a short time, the front door opened, my mother was home. My stepfather quickly pushed me away and zipped up his trousers – not quite understanding what had happened and still thinking it was a game, I excitedly started to tell my mother that Daddy let me play with his lily.

Then out of nowhere I felt an unmerciful slap across my face that lifted me clean off the floor. I turned to see my stepfather glare at me with pure fire in his eyes, a look that struck the divine fear of God into me. He bellowed at me to shut up and to leave my mother alone. I was very shaken, he grabbed me by the arm and dragged me into my room screaming at me to stay there until I was told I could come out. I sat on the floor and

CHAPTER 1: BEGINNINGS

sobbed. I was so frightened and I couldn't understand what I had done wrong. I mean I was only playing, so I thought. But something deep inside me told me I must never speak about this game. We played it many times after that.

Shortly after that we moved in with my stepfather's mother in Finglas. She was a scary, bitter woman who wore black-rimmed glasses and had long jet black hair that she wore in a tidy plaited bun. She was from Yorkshire, England, and although she had been in Ireland for many years, she never lost her strong Yorkshire accent. She hated my mother and I, referring to me as a bastard child which I never really understood at the time. She would give my mother a terrible time criticising her and making her cry. My mother was very obsessive about housework and Granny was the complete opposite. They would clash terribly over that. Granny had a dog, a little Yorkshire terrier called Pip. She loved it more than anything else in the world, buying the dog the best minced steak and feeding herself on very little. My mother hated this yappy dog with a passion and she would kick it at every opportunity she got, sending Pip yelping and crying to her basket.

Granny was a senior seamstress in a factory in Dublin city. One thing Granny did do for me which I will always be grateful for, was teach me how to handsew and use a sewing machine. She would go to work every day and my mother would have peace. My mother would spend the day cleaning and shouting at us to get out of her way. Then when Granny came home she would complain to my mother for touching things in the house, this went on daily.

When we lived in Finglas my mother would take and collect me from school because it was too far for me to go by myself. I did enjoy that, I enjoyed being like the other boys and girls, having my mum collect me, even though she was never really pleased to see me. I loved the walk home, walking up McKee Avenue and the different smells from the factories that lined both sides of the street. I don't remember too much else about that school other than that was where I was teased over my stammer.

I do remember taking part in the Irish dancing. We were practising for a show we were to put on one evening at school. I was really excited about this and when my mother came to collect me, I saw her across the street and without thinking I ran across the road and was hit by a car. I wasn't hurt, but I was a bit shaken up. I remember my mother screamed, and for that moment I believed that she did care about me. She was so lovely to me that day, she gave me a little hug, however small, it was a hug. We went back to the school that evening for the Irish dancing, and I lifted my legs high. I kept my hands by my side and my back straight and I danced for all I was worth. I caught my mother's eye and saw her laughing. I convinced myself she was really proud of me, but just didn't know how to show it.

Shortly after that day my mother was gone. We had no idea where she was and we were not told anything either. My stepfather stood Sharon, Patricia and I in the kitchen sink and washed us. He told us that we were going on a holiday. A lady known to us as Mrs Kelly came and collected us and took us away in her shiny red car. I later found out she was a social worker. She took us to a children's home on the south side of Dublin city – it was a huge, scary, cold, dark building with a sweeping staircase, the whole place had an eerie feel to it. I remember feeling very frightened, and Sharon and Patricia were

CHAPTER 1: BEGINNINGS

crying. We were met by two nuns who after a brief chat with Mrs Kelly took us into a huge room with four old roll-topped baths – they filled one of the baths with water and told us to get undressed. Patricia was crying really hard. One of the nuns grabbed her by the arm and glaring at her, told her if she didn't shut up crying she would give her something to cry for.

An instant fear set in for the three of us. Patricia very quickly stopped crying. We were scrubbed with carbolic soap, a smell I will never forget. When we got out of the bath our clothes had been taken away much to my horror – although my clothes were nothing much, they were mine. I was handed a navy blue corduroy dress with little yellow flowers on it. It had a big blob of blackberry jam on the front. I was horrified and remember being very upset, wanting my own clothes and feeling revolted that there was jam on the dress. I started to cry and the same nun who had grabbed my sister, grabbed me and screamed at me to shut up or I would be sorry. I remember I stopped crying straight away and tried not to let my quivering bottom lip show.

My sisters and I were then brought into a room full of other children of all ages. They were playing a game of 'ring-a-roses' with a nun who smiled at me and my sisters and invited us to play. Sharon seemed to be okay and didn't fuss, but Patricia was still very distressed. She was only three years old and clung on to me all the time. I remember feeling very protective toward both my sisters.

The time in the children's home was not the happiest of times, but it most certainly was not the worst either. As one of the older children there (being a worldly six years old) I was allowed to stay up a little later than the other children. We were brought into a room that had a small black and white TV and a wooden bench. Behind the bench was a large dining table with several chairs around it. We were put on the bench and warned not to look behind us – if we did, we would get smacked and put to bed. The nuns would sit behind us eating their dinner which smelt far nicer than anything we ever got to eat.

The Angelus would come on the small TV, we would fall on our knees and pray Hail Marys aloud until the Angelus finished. If we didn't do it properly we would be smacked and put to bed. It was so difficult as a small child not to look over our shoulders when the nuns were at the table – a knife would scratch on the plate or a fork would clink. It was torture not to look round when we heard a noise.

When the nuns had finished their dinner we would be brought in a line up to bed, to a large room with various iron-framed beds and cots. Sharon and I slept in beds and Patricia was in a cot. The nightime was the worst really – for some reason we would miss home, Patricia and Sharon would cry and I would try very hard not to cry, but sometimes I just couldn't stop myself.

Many children were like that, lots of us would cry when we went to bed. I would take Patricia out of her cot and get Sharon out of her bed and bring them into mine. The nuns used to get very cross, but they didn't do anything about it, so I just kept bringing them into my bed. Other brothers and sisters did the same.

Saturday was bath day, and all of us children would line up in the playroom as the bathroom was just off it. The four baths would be filled once and, starting with the youngest, eight children would be bathed at a time by the nuns. The water was never changed and we would still have to use it until everyone had been bathed.

CHAPTER 1: BEGINNINGS

Bath time was a very noisy time, children would be crying, nuns would be screaming at them to shut up, then there would be silence, the smell of carbolic soap heavy in the air, shiny faces and wet hair as we sat waiting to play 'ring-a-roses'.

One day Patricia was sitting on the floor on the other side of the playroom, and Sharon and I were playing with other children when I noticed Patricia was wriggling. I went over to the nun that was looking after Patricia and told her that she needed to go to the toilet. The nun ignored me and Patricia wet herself. I will never forget the nun giving Patricia such a slap across the face that she knocked her over. Patricia screamed as the nun grabbed her by the arm up off the floor and screamed at her that she was a 'pissy bitch'. I felt completely helpless, there was nothing I could do to help her. The nun took Patricia and put her in her cot, and I didn't see her until bedtime. I thought I would never get to bed to make sure she was okay. When I got to bed she was still sobbing – I picked her up, and saw the nun had put a terry nappy on her, which was soaking. I took her into my bed with Sharon and the three of us cuddled up and cried ourselves to sleep.

That was the worst thing that happened there, but it left us all quite traumatised. After that we just did exactly what we were told and tried not to upset the nuns.

Sunday was visiting day. We hadn't had any visitors as some children did. Then one Sunday, out of the blue we got a visit from Uncle Frank, my stepfather's brother-in-law. A larger than life character, he was an ex-army man who was a bit too fond of the drink, but I thought the world of him. He lived in Tallaght with my stepfather's sister, they had four children at the time, of similar ages to me and my sisters. We sometimes went to visit them and Uncle Frank would take us to the pub and buy us Fanta orange, a real treat. He also taught me how to scrum in rugby, he was passionate about the sport. I remember him singing 'My Ding-a-Ling' every time I saw him. I just thought he was great and secretly wished I had a dad like him.

So the Sunday he came to visit I was beside myself with excitement. We were allowed outside while he was there and we got to play on the swings. I remember him pushing us high on the swings and we giggled with glee. For that short time we were very happy. He produced a bag and placed it in my hand, I looked inside, it was full of sweets and chocolate bars. I showed my sisters, we had never seen so many sweets.

He gave us a hug and said he would come and see us again, but he never did. I will never forget him for that visit, he was the only person who came to see us the whole time we were there. When we got back inside with our big bag of sweets, excited I showed the nuns and the priest, he was there most Sundays. They all smiled and one of the nuns took the bag from me and said we could have the sweets later, she told me she would take the bag and mind it for us. I watched as she placed it in a cupboard in the corner, high on the wall, unreachable by little people like us. We never saw those sweets and chocolates ever again.

Then one day me and my sisters were called out of the playroom and there standing in the hallway were my stepfather and Mrs Kelly the social worker. My sisters were delighted to see them, they ran and gave my stepfather a hug, but I hung back, not sure if I was happy to see him or not. We were taken into the dreaded bathroom and scrubbed again, but this time we were given back our own clothes. I don't remember there

CHAPTER 1: BEGINNINGS

being a big farewell, nor do I remember saying goodbye to any of the other children.

Once we got in the car, my stepfather turned to us with a beaming smile and told us we had a new sister, and her name was Catherine. We were all very excited, when we got home there was my mother with our new sister in her arms.

For that very short time everything seemed almost great. But it wasn't long until things went back to the way they were. Now we were living in Granny's house my stepfather had to take me to the fields not far from the house to play his game. I didn't even hate it anymore. I would just do it because I had to, I didn't have any emotional feelings of any kind. I would just go into my dreamworld and pretend it wasn't happening.

Back at home all the fighting had started again. This time Granny had something else to throw at my mother, a new baby crying keeping her awake at night. One very wet cold day I remember my mother dragging all four of us girls on to the bus and arriving at Dublin Corporation. I remember the smell of the place and how old and dirty it was, full of people looking for housing.

We came out of the Corporation and walked for what seemed like ages to a block of flats in Dublin's inner city. I remember my mother being so excited as we entered what was a disgustingly dirty two bedroom tenement. It had a big front room with an open fire, a tiny dingy kitchen, two fair sized bedrooms and a dark horrible bathroom. My mother was so happy, and within a very short time we took residence of our tenement.

My mother worked hard to clean the flat and make it home. There was a second hand furniture shop in Parnell Street, and we would go to The Hill market every week. Bit by bit my mother managed to buy some things – one such thing was a beautiful radiogram. It was a piece of furniture in itself. She also managed to get a green leatherette suite, making our sitting room into, as we thought, a palace. Although we didn't have much food, and no luxuries like chocolate or biscuits, we had a very basic diet. My mother would go to Moore Street market every Saturday morning to get the best bargains in meat and veg she could.

Our tenement was situated just behind a very well known hotel in O'Connell Street. My mother would sometimes stand me outside the hotel on a Saturday morning to beg from the American and German tourists who stayed there. She would warn me that I had better come back with something or I would get a hiding. I remember standing there sometimes very cold, so cold I couldn't feel my fingers. I remember the tourists coming out of the hotel, the American men dressed in bright coloured clothes, some with chequered trousers and flat caps, the women dripping in gold with full makeup and brightly coloured lipstick. Their accents were only what I had heard on the TV. I thought these people were so rich, I thought their world was so far away from mine, I would stand there in awe watching them getting on their tour bus, hoping that they would notice me and give me a couple of pennies. Some days I would get more than others, after what would seem an age my mother would come and collect me. She wouldn't give me a hug or ask me how I was, she would just snatch the few pennies I had out of my hand and give me a slap across the head and tell me how useless I was. When we got home, my mother would sometimes light the fire to make the house 'cosy for your daddy' as she used to say.

CHAPTER 1: BEGINNINGS

Sometimes my mother would let me listen to the radiogram. On Saturdays it was storytime, and I remember sitting on the floor my hair covered in head lice lotion with my ear right up to the speaker listening to every single word of *The Lion, the Witch and the Wardrobe*. I thought it was the most amazing story I had ever heard and would tune in every week to hear the next part of the story.

For a time my mother and stepfather seemed happy. My three sisters and I shared a room, which was a bit cramped but we were all okay. Patricia slept in a single bed, Catherine slept in her cot and Sharon and I shared a double bed. Our bed had springs sticking out of it, and we would have to move our legs around to make sure we didn't get scratched, but of course once we were asleep our legs were all over the place and we would wake up with big scratches on our legs from the springs. Coupled with the scratchy black blankets from the Vincent de Paul and the itch of bed bug bites, sometimes getting to sleep could be very hard.

Being so used to hearing my mother and stepfather fighting, I would sometimes find it hard to fall asleep, frightened that the fights would start again. But for a while all I would hear was Jim Reeves and Johnny Cash records and sometimes the sound of my mother laughing.

We were sent to the local school which I enjoyed. My teacher was lovely, I don't ever remember her getting cross with me or with any of the other children. I remember we used to get our dinner in school, my favourite was sausage, mash, and beans, served in a tin foil tray. We got school dinners because most families in that area were so poor, school dinners were sometimes the only food we would have all day.

Imagine how delighted I was when I got chosen to play Mary in the Christmas Nativity, draped in blue crepe paper with Joey as my Joseph. Joey was a bit shorter than me with big brown eyes, and always looked like he needed a hair cut and a bath. He is the only person I remember from that school. We set off on our journey to Bethlehem from the back of the school hall, and as we passed all the mums and dads I remember feeling like a real star and not at all nervous. I caught my mother's eye in the audience and saw a smile that was quite alien to me, I was delighted that she was there. I had one line to say and decided right at that moment I was going to deliver it like I had seen Doris Day deliver lines in movies on TV, full of meaning, true Hollywood style. As we made our way to the stage, I turned to my audience and delivered my line in full voice: 'Joseph I am so tired!' Joey in turn, delivered his lines perfectly, as did all the other children taking part. I was delighted and believed there and then that I was destined to be a famous actress. But of course that was not to be the case.

Very soon after that, a man from Northern Ireland knocked on our door. I remember my mother bringing him into the sitting room and they stood and talked for what seemed like ages, as Sharon, Patricia and I played with baby Catherine, keeping her amused while my mother talked. A few days later there was a hive of activity in our flat – my mother and stepfather were rushing around hoovering and polishing the whole flat, shouting at us to keep out of the way. The man from the North was coming again, but this time he was bringing his new wife. Us girls were packed off to bed early, but we were too excited, no one ever paid us a visit. We went to bed and shortly after, we heard a knock on the door, followed by a loud unusual

CHAPTER 1: BEGINNINGS

laugh, a laugh like we had never heard before, then the beautiful English accent of a woman. We were all dying to get out of bed and see who this amazing sounding woman was, but we dared not for fear of a good hiding, so as the good girls we were, we fell asleep.

It was not long before we got to meet this woman with the amazing laugh and lovely English accent. She was the wife of the pastor at the Pentecostal church in Dublin city. They made a very attractive couple: she with long mousy hair, tall and very beautiful; he was tall, slim and devilishly handsome. They were very much in love and displayed their affection for each other openly. I thought they were so lovely and wished they were my mum and dad.

We started going to church every single Sunday. Saturday nights would be spent preparing: we would be scrubbed clean in the bath; shoes would be polished; hair ribbons ironed; my stepfather's suit picked up from the pawnshop, and taken straight back on Monday morning, a routine that was repeated each week.

I really enjoyed church. I loved to sing the hymns – I would sing loud and proud and for all I was worth – but the sermons scared me, basically we were all doomed if we did not ask Jesus to save us. My mother was the first one to be saved. She came back crying one Wednesday evening after prayer meeting, saying she had found Jesus and was saved. My stepfather very soon followed.

We lived in our tenement supposedly surrounded by the love of God and the church, and everything we did revolved around the Pentecostal church and the people who went there. My mother and stepfather became the socialites of the church, entertaining everyone, holding parties, holding prayer meetings. But there was no change in what was happening behind closed doors: my mother still beat me over the slightest thing; my stepfather still continued with his game. For me, things were to get a lot worse.

The usual thing would happen: I would lie frozen in my bed with Sharon sleeping next to me, I would hear his heavy footsteps outside my bedroom door, the soft voice saying 'Cassie, can you get up and make Daddy a cup of coffee?' Once I heard this I knew what was going to happen. When I brought his coffee to him he would be sitting on the chair masturbating. He would always say 'Look what Daddy has for you.' I would have to perform sex acts on him, my little throat would be so sore, I would gag and feel sick. Then his tone would change, he would firmly tell me to get back in to bed, and I would cry myself to sleep. This happened two or three times every week. Now my mother had found Jesus there was no stopping her going to prayer meetings, leaving me at the mercy of my stepfather. Then one night something happened which was to leave me traumatised for many years to come.

It started off in the usual way: my mother out, me in bed, my sisters sleeping, the voice at the door. I did what I was told, made his coffee and performed the sex act. But just as I thought it was nearly over, he pulled away and told me to sit on the sofa and open my legs – he started to touch me, I didn't like it and asked him to stop. But he wouldn't, he got cross and told me to shut up, and put his hand over my mouth. I saw fire in his eyes, and I was terrified. The next thing I knew, his big heavy body was on top of me – the horrible smell of diesel and BO was almost choking. He started pushing at me, tears streamed down

CHAPTER 1: BEGINNINGS

my face with the pain and fear and shock of what was happening. In my head I was screaming 'please Daddy stop, it's hurting' but he didn't stop, he kept pushing and pushing until I felt the most horrendous pain surging right through my little body. I tried to scream, but I couldn't, he pushed and pushed, I thought I was going to split in two, I thought I was going to die, my face wet with tears, but I didn't make a sound. I lay there in terrible pain frozen with shock. I wasn't able to go into my dreamworld that night – my whole body, my head, my heart, all felt broken.

When he had finished, he sternly told me to go to bed. I tried to get up, my legs like jelly, my body in pain from head to toe. As I looked over my shoulder at him, he sat back in his chair and lit a cigarette, avoiding my gaze. I climbed into bed next to Sharon silently sobbing. I was in shock, I couldn't believe or understand what had just happened, I was just eight years old. I cried like never before, until I finally fell asleep.

The next day I was so very sore and noticed I had big hand prints on my skinny legs and bruises on the inside of my thighs. I wanted to tell my mother. I wanted to scream to her what he had done to me, I wanted to scream so loudly how much I was hurting, I wanted to show her the marks on me, I wanted to sob in her arms and be held by her, I wanted to scream and scream, but I knew she wouldn't believe me, and if I told her she would blame me and I would get into terrible trouble.

I decided I just had to pretend it hadn't happened and I convinced myself it wouldn't happen again, but it did, over and over again until I was 16 years old. I became very good at detaching my head from my body when my stepfather was abusing me. I also learned to switch off when my mother and stepfather beat me. I would take my mind to anywhere I could. I would think about anything and everything other than what was actually happening – usually something nice like being a famous actress, or I would pretend that I had a different family that really loved me and that one day they would come and rescue me.

My saving grace was discovering the wonder and joy of writing. Writing opened up a whole new world to me. I couldn't or wouldn't dare express myself to my mother or my stepfather, but with the gift of writing I could be as free as a bird. I started to write fairy tales and little poems, and later on I would write songs.

Being able to write helped me so much to switch off from my reality. I would dream of the next thing I would write about. My mother would sometimes catch me dreaming and would beat me harder, calling me 'a deficient little bitch'. But I didn't care – there was one thing neither of them could take away from me, the love and excitement I had for writing.

Chapter 2

Responsibilities

1974 saw one of the worst bombings in Dublin's history and many civilians were killed. We were still living in our tenement. One Friday evening my sisters and I were sitting in our nightdresses watching TV, my mother was in the kitchen preparing dinner for my stepfather who was due home from work. All of a sudden there was a terrible bang. I remember my mother rushing out of the kitchen and looking out of the sitting room window. She never said a word until the second big bang, which was so loud that it made our flat shake. My mother screamed at us to quickly get outside. We, like every other person there, stood terrified as the cry 'it's bombs!' rang up and down the street. My mother was almost hysterical when the third bomb went off, and us kids were terrified to see all the grown-ups panicking.

My mother started to get really upset, as my stepfather was due home and was now late. She convinced herself that he must have got caught up in the bombs and was lying dead somewhere – my sisters were crying, but I remember I didn't cry. I was just looking around blankly at everyone being so hysterical, with the sound of fire engines and ambulances whizzing through the city almost deafening. My mother was being comforted by an elderly lady who lived in the neighbouring block of flats, she just kept calling my stepfather's name over and over again as she sobbed on this poor woman's shoulder.

Then out of the blue, there was my stepfather walking around the corner, fag in one hand, bike in the other. As he came towards us, my mother and sisters ran to greet him like some returning war hero. But my heart dropped when I saw him. I secretly wished he had been killed. I thought if he was dead then the things he did to me would stop. The reason he got home (as the story was told a thousand times) was because he had worked late and missed his normal train. If he had been on time he would have walked straight into the thick of the bombings.

It was a terribly sad day for Dublin – so many innocent people were lost, probably really good people too, and there was my stepfather, full of evil, still walking around with not as much as a scratch on him. Of course we had to go to church on Sunday and praise the Lord and say many Hallelujahs for my stepfather missing his train. The church said it was God's will, because my stepfather was such a 'good born again Christian'.

Life returned to normal after that, well, as normal as was possible for our family. People from the church seemed to be calling at our flat almost daily, one family in particular – the Murphys. They were older than my mother and stepfather and seemed to have taken them under their wing. They had three children the same ages as me, Sharon and Patricia. They were middle-class and living in Glasnevin in a very nice house. We used to visit them quite a lot and have the most lovely food: homemade jam, cakes, biscuits, lemonade, all the things we never had at home.

Mr and Mrs Murphy decided that our school was not suitable

CHAPTER 2: RESPONSIBILITIES

for us anymore. We were taken out and sent to a small Protestant school in Glasnevin. I quite enjoyed my time there. I discovered I was good at running. Being the fastest girl in my class, even though there were only five of us, that didn't matter to me, I was the fastest. I got to run in Santry Stadium for my school and I thought winning races was just the best thing. Running, like writing, gave me a wonderful sense of freedom, a feeling for me that was as precious as breathing.

Shortly after moving schools, we moved to a brand new house in Finglas, a move that was to intensify the abuse and fighting. I was given the box room at the front of the house, while my three sisters shared the big room. Now I was in my own room my stepfather had more freedom to abuse me, which he did regularly.

The church moved to South Dublin which made it more difficult for us to attend due to the cost of the bus fare, but we still went from time to time. Looking back, the Murphys were still taking an unhealthy interest in our family, they looked down their noses at us poor Moores, and yes we were poor, yes my mother suffered with her nerves, but their answer to everything was to praise God, yet everyone at the church was so busy praising God that no one saw the horrendous abuse that was going on right in front of their eyes.

It was decided that because we had difficulty in getting to church, prayer meetings should be held at our house. So Sunday evening was prayer meeting night. Some Sunday afternoons my mother would go out, and my stepfather would abuse me. I would then be told to get the chairs from the kitchen and bring them into the front room where a gathering of the born again Christians would be held. I would watch as my stepfather, the pillar of the church, would cry as he praised the Lord for all his glory. I would glare at him thinking 'bet you haven't told God what you did to me this afternoon' as I would shuffle on my chair sore from what he did to me that day. I would watch as all the people prayed and prayed, lifting their hands to heaven singing in a trance-like state – a really scary experience for a child. I would sit and pray from deep in my heart asking this wonderful almighty God, saver of souls, to 'please help me, please don't let Daddy come into my room.' But my prayers were never answered.

Despite this I totally believed in God, and I totally believed that the only way to heaven was to be saved so when I was 11 I was saved. I went to Sandycove to be baptised in the sea to wash away my sins. I was convinced that my life would get better, but it didn't and I didn't feel any different, nor did it take away the pain of what happened in the spring of 1976.

My mother decided to go to Canada to see her sister for three weeks, and we four girls were left in the care of my stepfather. It was a horrible time. He wasn't able to take time off work because we needed money. So I would have to get up at 6 a.m. to call him for work, I would then have to get my three sisters up and give them their breakfast (either two slices of toast or cornflakes – we were not allowed to have both). I would then have to clean out the fire, hoover and dust the house, then get my sisters ready for school, and head out with them to catch the bus to Harts Corner where we would walk down a long road to school. I remember seeing all the other kids being dropped off in cars by their mums – I always felt a little envious, seeing the other children being kissed and hugged, coming to school in nice clothes, carrying a nice school bag. Although always

CHAPTER 2: RESPONSIBILITIES

clean, we did not have nice clothes or nice school bags. We definitely looked poor, and most people at our Protestant school were well-to-do. Once we were in the classroom though none of those things mattered.

Those three weeks my mother was away I really struggled in school. I found it very hard to concentrate – with my mother away my stepfather was abusing me daily for hours. I daydreamed in school and I was so tired. I dreaded going home. When school was finished, we would walk to the bus, crossing back across the Harts Corner junction, a terribly dangerous road for four little girls to cross. I would hold on tight to my sisters' hands and, almost sergeant major-like, warn them to be careful. As I would turn the key in the lock my heart would sink knowing what would happen when he came home.

I tried to take my mind off things by being busy, I tried to do all the things I saw my mother do. The first thing I would do was light the fire and get the house cosy for my sisters, I would put them in the sitting room and put the TV on for them while I took on the Mummy role. I would have to cook dinner every day and have it ready for when my stepfather walked through the door.

I remember one day the Pastor's wife came round and showed me what to do if the chip pan caught fire. I watched intently as she demonstrated with a wet tea towel, then all of a sudden she burst into tears and said 'I can't believe I am showing a little girl what to do if the chip pan goes on fire.' She was so emotional she ran out of the house. I thought she was a bit crazy – I had already used the chip pan so many times. We mostly lived on sausages and rashers, mashed potatoes, beans or peas – that is all we could afford.

One day, I opened the cupboard under the sink and found pure orange juice, some small boxes of variety cereals and a few other 'luxury' foods, things that we never had. I sheepishly asked my stepfather about the stuff under the sink. He went mad at me, screaming that it was none of my business and how dare I look there. He gave me an awful hiding for that.

Later that week I found out he was having an affair with the woman next door, Jane Clark, a glamour-puss who loved herself, the complete opposite to my mother. He would sneak into her house after dinner and be gone for what seemed like ages saying she had a problem of one sort or another and he was going to help her. But it wasn't long before I realised what was going on, seeing the two of them giggling over the garden fence at each other.

But I decided I was going to keep the house nice for my mum, so when she came home she would be so proud and she would love me. One day I came home from school and did all the usual chores, but this day I decided to do the washing. I put all the clothes in the bath as I had seen my mother do a million times and I scrubbed them until my knuckles were sore. My small hands were not strong enough to wring the wet clothes out, so I did my best and put them into the laundry basket to take them downstairs and hang on the line. I was delighted with myself and thought my stepfather would be pleased and maybe he would leave me alone, and if Mammy saw me now she would be so proud. But the basket was too heavy for me to lift, so I thought 'well at least they are washed, Daddy can bring it downstairs when he comes home and then I will hang it on the line.'

My stepfather came home and as usual I put his dinner in

CHAPTER 2: RESPONSIBILITIES

front of him, and as usual he just grunted at me, not even looking me in the eye. I would then have to stand in the kitchen while he was eating and was not allowed to leave the room. All of a sudden he flung his chair back, picked up his plate and threw it at me. I nearly died with fright, not sure what was going on, then he grabbed my arm and pointing to the ceiling asked me what was that? I looked up and saw the drip of water coming down over where he was sitting. Forgetting about the washing I said I didn't know what it was. He dragged me upstairs and into the bathroom and then I remembered – 'oh Daddy, I did the washing, can you bring it downstairs so I can hang it out? The basket was to heavy for me?'

The next thing I knew I had a terrible pain in my ear and my face was burning and I was on the floor. He had given me such a slap across the face he had knocked me flying. He started screaming that because I didn't wring the clothes properly that's why there was water coming into the kitchen. I tried to protest that I had tried, but he was not having any of it, he picked up the basket and threw all the clothes back into the bath, screaming at me that I had made more work for him. He grabbed me again and gave me a terrible hiding with his belt.

Afterwards I sat in my room sobbing quietly, feeling so hurt physically and emotionally – I really thought I was doing a good thing and I had done my best. Later that night he showed me no mercy either.

A couple of days after that I thought I would wash the girls' bedroom floor. We didn't have carpet, just floorboards and lino, and the girls had lino in their room, so off I went and washed the floor as I had seen my mother do a thousand times before. I put the mop in the bucket, again my hands were not strong enough to wring out the mop, but I did my best. I was delighted with myself, thinking my stepfather would be pleased.

He had his dinner eating it like the pig he was, gazing at the half-naked woman in the newspaper he was reading. I remember being excited and nervous to tell him I had washed the floor, so I had to pluck up the courage. I very confidently told him what I had done, stupidly half expecting him to be pleased. Again he jumped out of his chair and started screaming at me that I was a stupid bitch, he was effing and blinding at me. I was terrified as he grabbed me by the arm and marched me upstairs and stormed in to the bedroom, all of a sudden his two feet went from under him and he fell flat on his arse on the floor. I couldn't help but have a silent giggle as I saw this big hairy lump sitting in a heap on the floor. Granted the floor was covered with puddles of water, but I did try my best – boy, did he give me such a hiding with his belt, saying I had made extra work for him and that I was useless. He threw me into my room. I sat on my bed sore from head to toe, but smiling through my tears at the memory of him falling flat on his backside.

Again that night he showed me no mercy.

A few days before my mother was due home my stepfather was spending more and more time next door with Jane. I didn't mind, because when he was there he was leaving me alone. One evening he came back from her house quite drunk – now as I said, my stepfather was not a drinker. I heard singing coming from the back garden so I went to investigate. I found my stepfather as drunk as a skunk sitting in the coal shed on top of all the coal. Quick as a flash, without thinking I slammed the door shut and locked him in. I was shaking from head to toe for being so bold.

CHAPTER 2: RESPONSIBILITIES

I went back into the house and hid behind the door, only to hear terrible banging and shouting coming from my stepfather. Scared, I didn't know what to do, so I went outside and stood at the coal shed door. He was shouting 'Cas, open this fucking door or I am going to kill you!' I replied, 'No Daddy.' This continued for a few minutes with him getting angrier and angrier, and me getting more and more scared. After a while he changed his tone and his voice became softer. 'Cas open the door please.' I refused because he would beat me, but he promised that he wouldn't. I made him promise again that he wouldn't be cross and he wouldn't touch me. He promised again. Believing him, I slowly opened the door, but I had no sooner shot the bolt when he grabbed me by the throat. I nearly died of fright. He carried me into the house by my throat and slowly took off his belt winding it around his hand buckle side out. He hit me so hard on my bottom and legs I had welts, and there was not a part of my body that was not deeply marked and sore.

He then grabbed me by the hair and dragged me upstairs flinging me into my room and slamming the door shut, shouting that he would be back. I sat in my room shaking and sobbing silently. I felt like I was broken, every part of me ached, my fingers were cut, my body was in pain and my head hurt from where he had grabbed my hair so tightly. I stayed in my room terrified. He did come back like he said and was so brutal with me.

The next day I got up as usual – I was in agony, the inside of me and the outside of me just felt broken to pieces and so sore. I tried to pretend I was okay and did all my chores, but every move I made sent pain shooting through my whole body.

I thought my mother would never come home: as bad as she

was I decided life was better when she was there. The day came to go and pick her up from the airport – we were so excited, we watched as she came through the terminal, she looked lovely, all suntanned in a nice summer dress, and we all ran to hug her which she responded to lovingly. I wanted to tell her straight away what had happened when she was away, I wanted to say 'Mammy when you were gone Daddy beat me so hard and he did terrible things to me, look at all the bruises I have.' I wanted to say this to her so much and for her to pick me up in her arms and hug me and to scream at my stepfather for hurting her little girl, but I knew that wasn't going to happen so I said nothing.

Instead when we got home I enjoyed listening to her stories of her time in Canada, for a few days she was lovely and I was in awe of her, but that was all to change when she found out my stepfather was having an affair with the woman next door. All hell broke loose, the fights were terrible, I would lie upstairs frozen to the bed with fear as crashing and banging and screaming went on for what seemed like hours.

The fighting escalated right up to the night of my tenth birthday, which had just been another day with no cards, no presents, no nothing. My mother and stepfather were having another horrendous fight, my mother was screaming at my stepfather 'don't tell her! Don't tell her!' I heard him marching up the stairs to my room. I was petrified as he burst through the door and just glared down at me – I didn't know what he was going to do. He leaned over me and said 'Cas, I am not your real Dad' before turning on his heels and walking out. I just lay there in shock. I had a feeling like someone was squeezing my insides and I couldn't breathe, tears welled in my eyes and I couldn't stop them as they rolled like a waterfall down my cheeks.

CHAPTER 2: RESPONSIBILITIES

So many questions ran through my mind and at the same time I felt I could answer most of them. Somehow things in my little head now made sense to me. I thought 'that is why my mother constantly calls me a mistake. That is why he did what he did to me. That is why they both beat me. I should not have been born.' I felt a sense of guilt for my very existence, but at the same time a huge feeling of anger swept right through me. I decided there and then that was why I was different to my sisters, and now I knew why I was different I would really detach myself from everyone. I would not let things upset me anymore. I would not look for approval or love anymore. I would just do what I was told and pray for the day when I was grown up and could leave, giving them a piece of my mind before I did so. Having decided all that I eventually fell asleep.

The next day my eyes were swollen from crying. I was in the kitchen making breakfast for my sisters when my mother walked in – I wanted her to hold me and tell me what my stepfather said was not true. I wanted her to notice my swollen eyes and broken heart, I wanted to talk to her about the night before. I wanted to ask her, if he was not my real Daddy, who was? But she didn't even look at me, she just scowled and made sure I did all my chores before I went to school. I gave my now half-sisters their breakfast, they were sitting at the table oblivious to what had happened the night before. As I looked at them I felt a huge sadness and pain in my heart, I could feel the tears welling again, but I knew I dare not let them spill over. If my mother saw me cry she would give me a hiding, so I swallowed hard and just got on and did what I had to do.

After that day I never quite felt the same. I became more dreamy and withdrawn at school, in fact I found school very difficult as I had all these things going around in my head that I found it impossible to concentrate properly. My teachers would get cross with me for my bad handwriting and at spelling I was dreadful. As for maths, well I hadn't a clue, all I saw when I looked at the page was lots of numbers and none of them made any sense to me. School became excruciating as I fell further and further behind.

My stepfather had a love of showing his authority, especially when it came to school, believing that he was a great scholar and knew everything, when that was not the case at all. Knowing I was really struggling, he and my mother used this to humiliate and torture me. Every now and again school bag inspection time would come around. I was not the tidiest of people when it came to my school bag, I would doodle on my books and would keep scraps of paper in my bag for ages. Because my handwriting was so poor, I was inclined to be very heavy on my pencil, causing it to show through on the page behind the one I had written on, so I would use the page opposite, leaving the one with the heavy marks blank. So when I would least expect it, I would be told to bring him my school bag, my heart would drop and I would feel sick because I knew what was coming. When I returned with my bag, my stepfather would be slowly taking off his belt glaring at me in such away that made me feel like I was going to pass out on the spot. My mother would be curled up on a chair by the fire smoking a cigarette, almost as if settling herself down for some sort of freak show. As my stepfather went through my bag I would be terrified, trying to remember if I did or had anything bad in there and at the same time trying to think of a good excuse to cover myself.

CHAPTER 2: RESPONSIBILITIES

The rules of the school bag inspection were that I would get three lashes of the belt across my bare bum for everything I did wrong – needless to say I would get many slaps and I would be screamed at for having papers in my bag, or not using the inside pages, or having doodled, or for having dog-eared books. I would be sobbing at this humiliation, it got even worse as my body started to develop. Standing there with a bare bum in puberty was just horrible. My mother would sit there watching everything almost enjoying this humiliation.

All this added to the difficulties I experienced at school. Thankfully there was one good thing, I had a very dear friend at school called Karen Pollard. Her family lived in a lovely large house, and I got to go there some days after school to play which was a real treat for me. It didn't happen very often, but when it did I loved it! Mrs Pollard was a wonderful woman and took me under her wing, she would genuinely be interested in what I had to say and was very caring. When I was there, I used to love the smell of home cooking and fresh baked cakes, the best smell in the world, and something I was not used to at all.

One day in August 1977, Mrs Pollard called to our house in Finglas. My sisters and I were outside playing – we used to play ball up against the wall, or get an old empty shoe polish tin and fill it with sand, and draw hopscotch on the ground and play for ages. On the day that Mrs Pollard came that is what we were playing while she spent ages chatting to my mother. The next thing I knew I was in the car with Mrs Pollard with a little bag packed on my way to Carlow for a holiday with Karen. Karen was already there staying at her grandma's, and Mrs Pollard thought it would be nice to bring me as a surprise to stay with Karen. Well, I had the best time ever, no one shouted at me, no one hurt me, no chores to do at all. Just able to play like the child I was. Mrs Pollard and her mother were just so lovely to me, I had the best food, things I had never tasted before, bedtime was a fun time, I got to brush my teeth every night without having to hide it. I even got tucked in when I went to bed, something that never happened in our house and boy did I enjoy every moment of it.

I learnt to ride a bike while I was in Carlow. I remember I couldn't wait to get outside each day after breakfast just to get on the bike, I practised and practised until my knees were cut and bleeding. I didn't care, I was determined to learn to ride it. I remember one evening it was getting dark, I was outside still trying to master the bike, Mrs Pollard and her mother were watching me from the kitchen window. They had asked me to come inside, but I begged them to let me try a few more times. As they were watching me I felt like the queen bee. I tried a few more times and then I got it… there I was, riding across the tarmac drive, a little wobbly but I was off. I don't think I was ever so delighted as I was at that moment. Mrs Pollard and her mother gave me a big round of applause with beaming smiles, and I thought I was going to choke on the pure thrill and delight I felt.

When I finally went indoors, Mrs Pollard sat me on the worktop and bathed my badly cut knees, I didn't care if it hurt, I could ride a bike and to me that was just the best feeling in the world. For the rest of the holiday Karen and I spent our time riding up and down the tarmac with such a sense of freedom and pure joy.

The day came when it was time to go home. For the whole week I had been in Carlow, I had had a taste of what it was like

CHAPTER 2: RESPONSIBILITIES

to be part of a loving family. As we pulled in to our estate in Finglas, my heart felt heavy, the feeling of fear set in and I felt sick as we walked up to the front door. Because Mrs Pollard was with me, we were met with a big smile from my mother, but as soon as she was gone the smile disappeared, and the first thing my mother said to me was, 'I hope you haven't bought home a load of washing for me!' I told her Mrs Pollard had done it all, she scowled and told me to go upstairs and clean my room. There was no 'how was your holiday?' or 'did you have a nice time?' so I didn't volunteer any information. I'd had a wonderful time and lovely memories, they couldn't take that away from me.

Karen and I ended up going to different high schools and we lost touch for many years, but I am happy to say we got back in contact a few years ago and remain good friends to this day.

I was no time home from my trip to Carlow, when things went back to exactly as they were before I went away, only they had intensified. My stepfather was still having an affair with Jane after promising that it was over. My mother was distraught. She called me into the kitchen one day, she was sobbing with a bottle of open tablets in front of her, she looked really drunk, her eyes rolling like she was going to sleep. I was so scared I started to cry with panic. She told me to go and phone the Murphys. I ran as fast as I could to the corner where the phone box was and rang them in a pure panic and told them that Mammy was crying and had taken tablets. They said that they would be around straight away and I was not to let her go to sleep. I ran back to the house and sat with my mother sobbing and begging her not to go to sleep. I just kept talking to her, about what I have no idea, I just kept talking. She was rambling about how she couldn't cope, and how terrible her life was.

The Murphys finally arrived and I was told to go back into the sitting room with my sisters. They came and told me they were taking my mother to the hospital and said I had to look after my sisters. I remember thinking 'here we go again'. I was so frightened, but also so angry with her. It wasn't the first time she had taken an overdose. How come no other Mammies did things like that?

My stepfather came home from work, but I was terrified to tell him what happened to Mammy. So I waited until he asked me where she was. I very sheepishly related the events of the day. He was furious – he slammed around, banging and crashing chairs, the table, anything he could, he slammed. Every slam made me jump with fear – not sure what to do I just stood there trying not to let him see how scared I was.

My mother returned a few hours later looking like a vision of death. She was accompanied by the Murphys. I was chased off to bed with my sisters, not having a clue what was going on. The next day as I did my chores before school, my mother briefly came downstairs to check I had done my chores properly.

She used to do that a lot, she would run her finger over the surfaces to make sure I had dusted properly, or she would walk around the kitchen with her head down checking to see if I had swept the floor thoroughly. If I had missed a bit she would give me such a clatter across the back of the head if I was lucky, but mostly she would grab the sweeping brush or the hair brush and hit me so hard until I fell to the floor – I had mastered the knack of curling up in a ball with my hands over my head when she did this. My fingers would be bleeding where she would try and get my head. Sometimes she would drag me to my feet by my hair and then really hammer me, if she used the hairbrush she

CHAPTER 2: RESPONSIBILITIES

would keep hitting me until the handle broke. I would always try to protect my head and that made her even more angry, she would be screaming at me that I was a 'lazy bitch' and how useless I was and what a mistake I was, with every slap she would tell me how much she hated me.

Sometimes she wouldn't let me go to school, she would keep me home to redo the housework, she would do things like tie terry nappies to my feet and get me to polish the kitchen floor over and over again, or do heavy manual work like clean the windows or scrub the floorboards on the stairs, and if my little hands couldn't quite get it right, she would hammer me again. I would be exhausted, broken, feeling like everything was my fault, like I was useless.

When we got in from school on the day after her suicide attempt, there was no sign of my mother. I went into the kitchen and found a note saying she had gone away for a while for a rest because she couldn't cope. My heart dropped when I saw the note, because I knew I would be at the mercy of my stepfather once again. This couldn't have been more true, she was gone for a week giving my stepfather a free hand with me, and boy, did he make full use of that time.

When my mother came home I wasn't delighted to see her, nor was I disappointed. By this time I had stopped having any real emotion, or any ability to show emotion – I felt, looking back, as if I was dead inside, no voice or ability to express myself, no tears to cry for all the hurt and pain I was feeling, no ability to feel anything.

Chapter 3

On The Outside Looking In

Not long after she returned, we were packing again to move. The affair with Jane proved too much for my mother to cope with, so in late 1977 we moved back to Ballymun, into a three-bedroomed first floor flat. Gone was our garden, although it wasn't big, it was a garden. We had moved to concrete city.

I was again given the small room by myself, and my three sisters shared the other room. Things were exactly the same when we moved there, the only difference was there was no upstairs to escape to when the fights started. One good thing was I was a little older and allowed to go out by myself to the shopping centre for my mother. I loved doing that, not necessarily the shopping but just to get out of the flat for a while. I would delay as much as I thought I would get away with, before I would go back up the piss-stinking stairs to our flat.

While in Ballymun, I became very involved with the church, and I would go out around the town with Dorothy and Rachel, two lovely ladies who took me under their wing and were leaders of a children's Christian group. We would go to different parts of Ballymun and preach the word of God to the children. Sometimes there would only be a few children, sometimes there would be a sea of kids, all sitting on the green space listening

CHAPTER 3: ON THE OUTSIDE LOOKING IN

intently to the lovely storytelling of bible stories. Dorothy would play the guitar and we would sing beautiful happy bible songs. I always felt great after singing, I would go home on a high, secretly wishing, hoping and praying that when I got home everything would be great, no more fighting, no more beatings, no more stepfather coming into my room. But no matter how good I was or how much I prayed it didn't stop.

The day came for me to start high school. I didn't want to go to that particular high school, but my mother being my mother insisted on sending me there. I hated it from the day I started until the day I left.

Firstly, most of the kids that went there were from well-to-do areas. We didn't have a uniform which was excruciatingly difficult for those of us who came from a less privileged background. I had one outfit of clothes, a blue A-line skirt, a white cheesecloth blouse, and a pair of black platform shoes, which my big toe had poked a hole in. I would wash out my clothes every night by hand and dry them on the floor ready for the next day, but of course I was teased desperately at school, I was called smelly because I always wore the same clothes. I would put black boot polish on the toe of my sock to try and hide the fact that I had a hole, but through the course of the day my sock would move and the hole would become so obvious.

Having started my periods I put on weight, and I had terrible acne on my face especially on my forehead. My mother insisted that I wore my greasy hair off my face revealing this horrendously raw acne. She used to find it funny that I looked so ridiculous and took great joy in laughing at me. I became increasingly awkward, withdrawn and desperately uncomfortable about myself when I hit puberty, I hated everything and everyone and most of all, I hated myself. My stepfather continued to abuse me, but I started to protest that I didn't want to do it anymore. He would get angry and threaten to get one of my sisters to do it if I didn't and would say 'how would you feel about that?' I felt sick at the thought of them having to go through the same, so I would just have to carry on.

Life at that time was as bad as it could get for me. School became impossible, I couldn't manage the work at all and I couldn't concentrate. I was so far behind with my work, because of all the stress I was under at home, and there was not a soul I could talk to or tell.

I would go to school and see everyone else happy, messing around, having fun. I felt invisible, I would just walk around the school by myself, until I got in with what I thought was the cool gang. We started smoking thinking we were so grown up. I was desperate to be accepted and if they said 'jump' I would have asked 'how high?' Even though deep down I knew they were not very nice to me, I accepted it all just to be part of something.

One day the 'rag bag' arrived at our house, something that happened a couple of times a year. It was a bag of clothes that would be donated to us by the church. It was called the 'rag bag' because most of the clothes in there were nothing more than rags. But this bag was different, in it was a pair of denim jeans, and although they were very flared jeans, I didn't care, they were jeans as far as I was concerned. I came up with a brilliant idea – my mother was out at an antenatal clinic as she was pregnant again, so I decided while she was out I would make these jeans into the best jeans ever. I would go to school and I would be

CHAPTER 3: ON THE OUTSIDE LOOKING IN

just like all the trendy girls. I took them into my room, cut open the seams, and sewed them back up again to be drainpipe jeans just like all the other girls had.

I was delighted with myself, I thought I was gorgeous. Next day, off I went to school in my drainpipes. I travelled on the bus, I walked up the road to school, I got into my first class, and as I sat down the two seams of my jeans burst open right up to the crotch. I was mortified, everyone in the class laughed at me – at that very moment I wanted to die right there on the spot. The teacher told me to go to the Home Economics teacher and get her to fix my jeans. Mrs Richards was a scary sullen-faced teacher, who, when I explained what had happened, looked at me in pure disgust, and told me to get into bed in the sick bay. I climbed onto the bed and covered my legs with a blanket as she took my jeans away.

While I was lying there, I consoled myself with the thought that at least Mrs Richards would make a proper job of my jeans, and I could claw back some dignity. I was feeling quite pleased at that prospect. When Mrs Richards arrived back with my jeans however, I was horrified to see that she had sewn them back up exactly as they were when I got them out of the rag bag. I was mortified at the thought of having to go around wearing these hideous flared jeans. Crippled with shame and total humiliation, I wandered back to my class and for the rest of the day I had people pointing and laughing at me, some looked at me in pity, it was horrible, totally horrible. Needless to say I never wore those jeans ever again.

Although I hated school and I really struggled, I dreamt of being a doctor. I really believed that I would go to college and become a great doctor, but that was never to be. My days at high school were less than happy for me, made much more difficult of course by the endless stress and abuse that was going on at home. But little did I know, that over the next couple of years, the events that were to come would change my life forever.

Chapter 4

'Mammy, I'm Bleeding'

My mother and stepfather had met a young widow called Grace, she had three little girls and lived in a small flat on the other side of Finglas. I started to babysit for her from time to time, and she became friends with my mother and stepfather spending quite a bit of time with them. By this time my mother had another baby, Sheila, who was beautiful, but boy, did she cry a lot! So my mother depended on me more and more while she nursed Sheila.

One day Grace invited our whole family down to the countryside for a holiday on her parents' farm. We were so excited, we had never been on a farm before, in fact I thought I would burst with excitement. It was Whitsun and the weather was lovely. We headed out to the countryside on the bus, and we were met by a lovely jolly smiling woman who greeted us warmly – Mrs Rodgers was her name. She collected us in her small car, all seven of us squashed in. She took us to what I can only describe as the biggest house I had ever seen in my whole life. We pulled in through a huge set of iron gates and drove up a beautiful, sweeping, tree-lined driveway. The sheer size of the house was mind-blowing to us kids. The smell of the farm was totally alien to us, but there was something very comforting about the smell. I have to say it beat the smell of piss that we were used to in Ballymun.

As we stood at the enormous front door Mrs Rodgers welcomed us to her wonderful home. When we entered the house I could not believe my eyes, I expected maids and butlers to come running to take our bags, just like I had seen on the TV. It was like our whole flat would fit in the hallway alone.

We were taken upstairs and shown our rooms – it was so exciting, I felt I was in a movie. Sharon and I were sharing a room, it was Mrs Rodgers' son's room, she told us his name was Jim and he was away for the weekend, so that is why we could have his room. Sharon and I were delighted. The view from the window was amazing, looking over fields, and seeing cows everywhere was just the best thing.

We had a lovely weekend there, wandering around the huge farm, seeing all the animals, tramping through the fields, eating the most amazing home-cooked food and lots of it. Mrs Rodgers was the most amazing cook, she was a dream Granny fussing over us girls like she had known us all our lives. We enjoyed every moment. We had great fun with Mr Rodgers who was a large jolly man who loved to tell stories and I would love to listen, hanging on every word. He would dress in a cotton shirt with smart trousers held up with braces, something we had never seen before. He had the most amazing handlebar moustache, and I was fascinated to watch him as he would sit at the big kitchen table and twirl the sides of his moustache so it would sit under his nose with a curl on each side.

It was just the best weekend ever, for that time we seemed like a normal loving family, something I desperately wanted to

CHAPTER 4: 'MAMMY, I'M BLEEDING'

last when we got back to Dublin. God, would I never learn? That definitely was not going to happen.

We returned to Dublin and within days the countryside was a distant memory, it was like I dreamt we went there. But much to my delight Mrs Rodgers came to visit during the summer holidays, and asked if she could take me and my sister Sharon back to her house for a holiday. We couldn't believe that my mother agreed. We set off in the car with Mrs Rodgers – the journey seemed endless, although Mrs Rodgers chatted to us the whole time, I just couldn't wait to get there. When we arrived and got out of the car, I can remember getting the most amazing feeling of warmth and excitement as I breathed in the lovely country air, I felt like all my fears and pain had melted away.

Sharon and I had the best time ever, we were spoilt rotten, we cooked, laughed, played, ran and just had a wonderful time. We had a bath every day, and I remember the smell of 'Head and Shoulders' shampoo. It smelt so lovely, better than the washing-up liquid we had to use at home. I remember my cheeks feeling warm and looking as red as cherries from all the air, even my acne had cleared up a bit.

Jim was there this time, he was in his mid twenties and almost bald. He was by no means a handsome man, but he gave me lots of time, and he didn't mind me following him around like a puppy dog every day. I wanted to bring the cows in to be milked, I wanted to see the cows being milked, I wanted to see and be part of everything that was going on, and at no point did he object or get impatient with me. When we were finished on the farm, we would go into the lovely warm kitchen, the smell of a wonderful dinner wafting from the Aga, and a wonderful sense of happiness gripped me like I can't explain. Sharon wasn't really interested in the farm, she much preferred to stay with Mrs Rodgers cooking and shopping. That was something I did every day in Dublin, but I was glad to escape from it when I was in the countryside.

Dinner time was chat time – Sharon and Mrs Rodgers would tell us about their day, and at a hundred miles an hour I would tell them all the things Jim and I had done on the farm. Sharon and I experienced love and warmth like never before, so much so, Mr and Mrs Rodgers treated us as if we were their own grandchildren. I thought I would burst with happiness that week, it was just wonderful, my cheeks hurt from smiling all the time, life in Dublin seemed to fade quickly away for that short time. What I didn't realise was there was a bigger plan for me.

The day came when Sharon and I had to return to Dublin, heartbroken and sobbing – we did not want to leave this wonderful life. Mrs Rodgers assured us that we would be coming again on our next holiday. Just as we were getting ready to leave, Mrs Rodgers called me to the sitting room and closed the door, she handed me a bag and told me she had sent away to England for what was inside. I opened it to find an array of creams and lotions. She very gently and lovingly explained that it was for my acne. I was so touched that she would do that for me.

Heading back to Dublin, I could feel all the feelings of fear and heaviness coming back, having experienced such a happy time, I realised I wanted that all the time. Back at home it was not long before the memories of that summer week in the countryside faded. Back to the beatings, back to the shouting, back to the horrendous abuse, back to struggling at school. I so hated my life.

CHAPTER 4: 'MAMMY, I'M BLEEDING'

At the ripe old age of 13, my mother told me I had to go and get a job. There was no way that she could afford to keep me at school now she had another baby. Although I hated school and wasn't very good at it, I really wanted to stay and get some qualifications to help me to get a good job. I decided to ask in every shop in Ballymun shopping centre.

One shop in particular I kept asking was a paper shop, it was one of the busiest shops in the centre, they sold practically everything from cigarettes to ham to toys. The owner was very good to everyone, allowing a certain amount of credit. People loved him. Most times I asked him for a job he would very kindly smile at me and tell me I was far too young, but I was very persistent. I think he got fed up in the end and just gave me a job! I started in the August, just after my 13th birthday, on Friday evenings, all day Saturday and all day Sunday. I received £12.50 a week. I was delighted, I felt so grown up, I believed I would receive some respect now I was working. How foolish can a child be?

I loved my job, my boss was a gentleman to work for, and the other girls that worked there, although older than me, were very nice to me too. I would get paid on Sunday evenings, and delighted with my £12.50 I would head home only to have my money for a very short time. My mother would be waiting for me to come home and she would take £10 a week from me, telling me I had to pay my way now I was working. I didn't mind too much, but sometimes I felt a bit fed up. I used my £2.50 for the bus fare to get to school.

Christmas of that year turned out to be one of the best I ever had. My sister Sharon was the blue-eyed girl in the family, she was very academic, and as my mother would say 'not an ounce of trouble, unlike Cassie'. Funny, I don't ever remember being troublesome. Sharon wanted a guitar for Christmas, I didn't ask for anything convinced I would get little or nothing as usual. Christmas morning came and lo and behold I got a guitar too. Now it was nothing fancy, just from a cheap shop in Ballymun, a small nylon-stringed guitar, but I didn't care – it was the best present I ever had.

I took my guitar into my room and I sat for what seemed like hours trying to get a tune from it. I was delighted with myself when I managed to play what I thought sounded like the theme tune to *Tales of the Unexpected*, a TV show that was on in the late 70s and early 80s. It probably sounded nothing like it, but to me it was just pure class. I practised and practised until the tips of my fingers were so sore, but I was determined to learn how to play. In my mind I was thinking not only may I become a famous actress, but now I could become a pop-star with my guitar. Anyone I met who played the guitar, I tormented to show me chords. I managed to string a few chords together and create what I thought was just brilliant. To have music while I sang was just the best thing. It wasn't long until I started writing my own songs.

I wrote my first song when I was 13, I'd had a terrible beating over something or nothing again, and was as usual sent to my room. I remember it was a beautiful sunny evening, I could hear children playing outside, cars and buses going up and down the road, life seemed to be going on as normal for everyone around me. I felt that my life was stopping, I felt more alone than I had ever done before.

I remember feeling very angry this particular evening, it was like something deep inside me swelled up. I can't explain it very

CHAPTER 4: 'MAMMY, I'M BLEEDING'

well, but it was like a true defiance, and I swore to myself that evening that when I grew up I would never live the life of my mother and stepfather, I would never treat anyone as I had been treated. I would be everything that my mother was not, and I felt brief elation at what I visualised for my future as an adult.

I picked up my guitar and wrote, 'Do You Feel Lonely?'

> Do you feel lonely and nobody cares?
> Do you need someone but there's nobody there?
> Just turn to Jesus he loves you,
> Just turn to Jesus he'll always be true.
>
> Do you feel like shouting but no one can hear?
> Do you feel like crying but can't shed a tear?
> Just turn to Jesus he loves you,
> Just turn to Jesus he will always be true.

I was so pleased with that song I sang it over and over again. Sometimes after my stepfather abused me or I would have had a beating from one of them, I would play that song and sing through blinding tears, my heart feeling like it was being ripped out, I would plead with God to please make all this horrible stuff stop. I would sometimes wonder what I was doing wrong that my prayers were not being heard.

But I would continue to write Gospel-type songs using the three or four guitar chords I had, trying to get a different sound for each song. I loved it! Nothing could compare to the wonderful world of writing and music. I thought for a while I was in control of things, in that I was working, I was writing songs, I was going to church, I was going to the farm for most of my holidays. Things seemed to be looking up, even though the abuse was still continuing from my mother and stepfather, it seemed to drift almost in to insignificance. I was able to switch off and dream of the next song I would write, or the next visit I would have to the farm or my next week's money. There was so much more I could think of, and all of it was good.

Then, when I was 14 one Saturday when I was working, I had my period. I was so ashamed and disgusted at it, and found it a total inconvenience. My mother had never told me the facts of life, nor did she tell me about periods or how to look after myself. The day I started my period I though I was going to die, I had been swinging on some railings and banged myself hard. When I came home I was bleeding and I started to cry. I called my mother in panic and told her I was bleeding, she just laughed and threw me in what looked like a nappy and told me to put it inside my knickers. That was the only time she gave me any help. So like with most things in life at that time, I chose not to think about it too much.

This particular Saturday, I started to get the most horrendous cramps in my stomach. I went to the toilet and found I was bleeding very heavy. I had nothing with me, so I folded up some toilet paper and put it into my knickers and hoped for the best. I tried to keep working and pretend I was okay, but the pain was so bad and I could feel myself leaking. I had no choice but to ask to go home. My boss could see I was not well at all and told me to go.

I remember walking across the field to our flat and thinking I was never going to make it with the pain. It was by the grace

CHAPTER 4: 'MAMMY, I'M BLEEDING'

of God I got home. When I got indoors, my mother came into the hallway, I was doubled over feeling like I was going to pass out. She started shouting at me asking what the hell I was doing home? I tried to tell her I wasn't well and that I was bleeding very heavily. She got very impatient with me telling me I was a drama queen, she told me to go into the bathroom and sort myself out and started shouting at me for having blood on the back of my skirt. She followed me into the bathroom shouting at me, while I sat on the toilet. The pain was like my worst period ever, I felt like I was passing my whole insides, I wanted to scream out loud, but I dared not for fear of another hiding.

I thought the pain would never go away. I stayed in the bathroom for what seemed like ages until eventually the pain did subside a little. I was still feeling very unwell and bleeding heavily. I cleaned up as best I could. I came out of the bathroom and my mother was in the sitting room drinking coffee and smoking a cigarette. I sheepishly went into the room and she started shouting at me that I had better have cleaned up my mess properly, she told me she did not want to see anything left after me and if my stepfather saw anything she would kill me. She warned me never to breathe a word to anyone about what had just happened. I wanted to scream at her, 'Mam I am not well, I am frightened, am I going to die?' but I knew she didn't care and I knew she would not answer me. So I didn't say a word. I had to carry on as normal and do all my chores. I thought bedtime would never come so I could lie down.

Some years later I was to get the same pain, only then could I make sense of what happened that day, and why my mother was so aggressive towards me. I realised I'd had a miscarriage.

Chapter 5

A Schoolgirl Crush

When I was 15 years old we moved again, this time to what might as well have been the other side of the world to us, we moved to Tallaght. Having always been on the north side of town, Tallaght seemed like the middle of nowhere, and to be honest it was a bit like that when we moved there. Although we had a shiny brand new 4-bedroomed house, we were on the side of a mountain in the middle of a building site with little or no infrastructure, on the south side of the city. The place was almost alien to us.

We still had to travel to the north side for school, that journey every day was murderous, and by the time I was 15 I had fallen so far behind I really couldn't see the point of going anymore. School for me by this time was just pure agony. I got a full-time job in a local shop which my mother thought would be a great idea. I was delighted, no more school. I was now a full-time worker, I was a grown woman (as I thought) and it wouldn't be long until I could save up enough money to move out, and once and for all I would be free. I could do, and have anything I wanted now I was working. How foolish can one be?

The trips to the countryside were becoming more frequent. Jim had started showing an interest in me, which I found very

CHAPTER 5: A SCHOOLGIRL CRUSH

flattering. He started to come to Tallaght once a week usually on a Sunday, he would take me out and we would go to a local hotel and have a drink. I was convinced I was so grown up. I had a job, and even though my mother took most of my wages it didn't matter. I was working, I was out of the house away from my mother and less accessible to my stepfather, and although he did still abuse me whenever he got the chance, I didn't care anymore. I held on to the fact that I was getting older and soon I would be out of there. I now had a boyfriend, I could have a drink and smoke cigarettes, I mean how grown up is that?

Jim and I got on very well, I really looked forward to him coming up on Sundays and I loved our evenings out. We would have a kiss and a cuddle and he would grope at me, but I didn't know what was right and what was wrong so I did what I thought was expected of me. Even with Jim I would switch off when he would touch me, nothing had any meaning for me it was just routine, just what was expected.

We saw each other for almost a year, he coming to Tallaght every week, me going to the farm whenever I had time off – life seemed good. Having Jim in my life was a huge escape from what was going on at home.

When I turned 16 I lost my job – I was upset, no more escape, stuck at home with my mother all day, it was horrible. Then one Sunday, Jim came to visit, he told me that a woman down the road from him was looking for someone to clean her house and look after her children, he said I could live at the farm and work for this woman. I thought I was going to burst with excitement at the thought of finally being free, away from my mother, away from my disgusting stepfather, this was like God was finally answering my prayers. Jim spoke to my mother, and to my complete shock and surprise she, without hesitation, agreed to let me go. As quick as anything I ran upstairs and packed my bag, not that it took me too long as I had little or nothing to pack. As I was throwing things in my bag, I was so excited I was shaking, I remember saying 'thank you God, thank you God' over and over again.

Life was now looking up. Mr and Mrs Rodgers were so loving and kind to me. I would go to my work which I enjoyed very much, and when I came home I arrived to a warm loving welcome and a beautiful hot meal, something that I had never had before. When I wasn't working I would be outside on the farm, wellingtons on, mucking in, doing whatever needed to be done, I loved it. When I wasn't outside Mrs Rodgers would teach me how to cook all the meals that she prepared, like delicious casseroles, roast dinners, or baking brown bread.

Jim and I continued with our courtship, which looking back for me wasn't anything more than a silly schoolgirl crush, but I enjoyed the attention that he showered on me, blinded by the fairy-tale feeling of everything. I really started to feel I was grown up and the abuse and terror that I had experienced was well behind me. Jim would take me to my mother's every Sunday, I felt amazing knowing that she could not touch me, nor could my stepfather. I guess I was going through the rebellious teenager years but didn't know it, I did feel quietly conceited. What I did notice when I would go to my mother's was that my beloved sisters had become very cold towards me, almost as if they really disliked me. I was a little upset by their attitude, but lost in the joy of my new life so I didn't heed it too much, something I was to regret deeply for many years.

CHAPTER 5: A SCHOOLGIRL CRUSH

By January 1983, I was as happy as I thought I could ever be – life was sweet and I was not living in fear anymore. I felt I had the life that I had dreamt of when I was a little girl. I was still a dreamer, I would pretend in my head that this was my real home and that this was my real life, the life I left behind was just a mistake, just one of those things and this is where I really belonged. My mother got a phone in her house and with the novelty of it, would ring me every day with news of some disaster or problem she had. I used to get annoyed, but consoled myself that she was on the other end of the phone, so there was not a lot she could do to me, only make the odd hurtful comment, and there was not a lot I could do for her, only pretend I was concerned for her woes. When I'd finished talking to her, she always asked to speak with Mrs Rodgers or Jim. I would skip off and find something to do, glad to get off the phone – little did I know what they were planning and what was about to happen.

In February of 1983, on a visit to my mother's, I was told to go and see my sisters upstairs for a while, my mother, stepfather and Jim wanted to talk. Totally oblivious to what was going on, I willingly did what I was told. I went to see my sisters and was greeted with such hostility from them, they told me they hated me along with a few other choice words. I asked them why they were saying such things and they replied 'you don't care about us anymore, now you have moved out you think you are something special.' They told me that they had to do all the chores that I had done and my mother would tell them they were useless, and that they couldn't do it as well as I did. I was so upset. My mother had turned my sisters against me in making out I was the golden girl, when in actual fact she couldn't stand me. She had succeeded in driving a wedge between me and my sisters.

I didn't get much of a chance to explain things to them as I was ordered downstairs by my mother. I walked into the kitchen and saw in my mother's hand a piece of paper, and she was waving it at me with a big beaming smile. I didn't understand what was going on. Jim and my stepfather were standing shoulder to shoulder with big smiles on their faces, and my mother not able to contain her excitement any longer blurted out to me that I was getting married. What she had in her hand was a marriage consent form which they had to sign because I was only 16 years old, I wasn't old enough to make that decision myself and I needed parental permission. She showed me their signatures. I didn't know what to say, but I went cold with shock. Jim had joked around saying he was going to marry me, but I hadn't taken him seriously.

My mother handed Jim the signed consent form and turned to me and told me to go and peel the potatoes for dinner. The three of them sat on the sofa and chatted, as if I wasn't there. I stood with my back to them peeling potatoes. I don't think I ever peeled potatoes so fast in all my life.

A steam train was running though my brain and I was trying hard not to cry, I mean I was only 16, I was very fond of Jim but far too young to love him or know what love was. I just thought: I want to go dancing, I want to earn enough money to live by myself, I want to do all the things I had seen other single girls doing. Then the other side of me thought: I love the farm, maybe it won't be that bad after all to be married. I just couldn't think straight. I remember the sound of the three of them laughing and joking, full of merriment as they whispered and chatted.

CHAPTER 5: A SCHOOLGIRL CRUSH

On the way back to the farm in the car Jim was excitedly talking about the wedding and working out dates, it had been decided that we would not have a long engagement and that a spring wedding would be a good idea. He told me he would take me to Dublin during the week to get me an engagement ring. I tried to pretend that I was excited, but inside my heart was breaking – as I looked at Jim I knew there and then that I most certainly did not love him.

When we got home he went straight to the kitchen where his mother and father were, and holding my hand, he with a huge beaming smile announced that we were going to get married. His parents were delighted. It was agreed that Jim would go and see the minister of the church to make arrangements. It was also agreed that the wedding reception would be held in the house as it was so big there was plenty of room to have a crowd. We went to Dublin and got the ring something I wasn't really bothered about. Jim was very money conscious so he did not buy anything fancy, in fact he bought the cheapest ring he could find. I do have to say when I saw it on my finger I did get a little excited, I never had any jewelry before, this was my first piece and as it sparkled on my finger for a little while I felt good, as I showed if off to anyone who would look at it.

All the arrangements were made between my mother and some ladies from the church – no one asked me what I wanted, or how I felt.

A spanner was thrown into the works so to speak, and Jim came storming in one day cursing and swearing, scratching his head as he often did, he was furious. He had been to see the minister who had in no uncertain terms refused to conduct the wedding ceremony on the grounds that I was only 16, in his opinion far too young and secondly I was not a Protestant. I couldn't help but have a small smile of relief. I sat very quietly while Jim ranted and raved. It was then decided that we would get married in a solicitor's office, with a commissioner for oath. I was gutted: whatever might have been good about getting married in a church, I couldn't see anything nice about getting married in a solicitor's office. However, I didn't say a word, I just went along with everything that was happening. I convinced myself that I was away from all the abuse, so this had to be better and it was God's way of taking me away from that situation.

The date for the wedding was set for April. Two weeks before the wedding it was decided that I should go back home to Tallaght to be fitted for a dress. What I didn't know was I wasn't getting a new dress, my mother and Mrs Murphy had asked around all their recently married friends for the loan of a dress. Eventually one was found – a lady in her late thirties had got married the year before and was only too delighted to let me have her dress. I tried it on and it fitted badly – it was far too loose and way too long, but all agreed it was fine. I looked in the mirror, dressed in a long white hideous dress and an even more hideous veil and thought I looked dreadful. I hated it so much. This is not what I had dreamt of, I dreamt I would look like a princess, I dreamt I would have the dress of my dreams, I dreamt I would look and feel like one of the beautiful brides I had seen on the TV or in a fancy magazine. The girl looking back at me in the mirror was very far from a princess, I looked like a really badly made white meringue. I wanted to scream at my mother and Mrs Murphy, telling them I hated it, telling them that it was hideous, but I dared not say a word. The woman who let me borrow the dress very excitedly told me how

CHAPTER 5: A SCHOOLGIRL CRUSH

she'd had it made and all the detail and decision making that went into it, but no matter how much passion she had for her dress, that's exactly what it was, her dress not mine, so I couldn't feel any of the passion she felt, all I could feel was pure despair and disappointment.

The two weeks I spent in Tallaght were horrible. I didn't get beaten, but my mother couldn't help herself from making mean nasty comments about things like my weight or my acne, or telling me what a disappointment I was and how much she had sacrificed for me, just generally making me feel as she always had, like I was nothing. She also made a comment that didn't make any sense to me at the time: 'the money we got will never be enough for what you put me through!' I hadn't a clue what she was talking about or what she meant, what money? I did notice that there were changes in the house – a new kitchen, a fancy new cooker, the house was decorated from top to bottom with new carpets throughout. But I just assumed my stepfather was doing well at work. I was to find out on my wedding day what she meant, and exactly where all the new stuff for the house had come from.

During those two weeks, my stepfather was to abuse me for the last time. I remember thinking about that fact, as he was abusing me, and feeling this huge surge of anger tinged with delight at the thought he would never get the chance to do this to me again. He made me promise that I would allow him to continue after I was married, I did promise, but in my heart I was screaming 'Never! Never! Never!' As I pulled up my knickers and walked away, I decided there and then that getting married was probably a good thing for me, at least I would be well away from him and he could never abuse me again.

The day of the wedding arrived and as I woke up at the farm, I heard the hive of activity buzzing around the house. I laid there as the sun streamed in the window with tears in my eyes and a very heavy heart. I could hear people laughing and talking and all I wanted to do was curl up, put the blankets over my head and hope that they would all go away and this was just a bad dream. I didn't feel excited anymore, I just felt pure panic at the thought of what lay ahead for that day. I stayed in bed wrestling with my thoughts and trying not to cry. Jim had told me the week before the wedding that he had sold almost all of the farm animals and machinery, he explained he was going to lease out the land and live on the profits. He had made some bad business decisions and had no choice but to sell everything off. I was devastated – my beloved cows and tractors all gone.

As I lay there, thinking about everything and wanting to die, my mother came bursting in the room telling me to get up. I dragged myself out of bed and wandered down to the kitchen, there was cooking and baking going on, everyone was so busy, everyone was rushing around, Jim and my stepfather were busy moving furniture around, all the children were running around and playing. I remember feeling like I was invisible, I was watching all this going on and feeling nothing, feeling like I wasn't part of it.

My mother came and shouted at me to hurry up and have a bath as we had to be at the solicitor's office at 11 a.m. It was decided that Mr Murphy and Grace would come with us as our witnesses. I was hearing all these things going on and arrangements being made, but not really caring or understanding what was happening. My heart was too heavy to care. I sauntered upstairs and had my bath, I remember putting

CHAPTER 5: A SCHOOLGIRL CRUSH

my head under the water to drown out the noise of everyone downstairs, and a voice was screaming inside me 'I don't want to do this!'

The next thing I knew I was standing in the living room dressed in a suit consisting of a cream jacket and a cream and burgundy-checked pencil skirt with a matching scarf. I looked like I was 60, not 16. It was decided that I should not wear the wedding dress to the solicitor's office because it would draw too much attention, I should wait until I got back and wear it then. It had been decided that we would have a blessing ceremony in the house conducted by Mr Murphy.

As we headed off to the solicitor's office in the old car, I remember thinking 'Is this it? Is this really my wedding day?' No ribbons on the car, no flowers, no nothing, just me and my future husband, Mr Murphy and Grace heading out in silence to the solicitor's office. We arrived at this dark, dingy, untidy office full of stacked files on the floor, and a bespectacled, tall, thin man greeted us and read out some cold legal jargon that I had not a clue about. When asked to say yes I did, and before I knew it, that was that, a wedding band on my finger and we were married. No church organ, no smiling faces, no congratulations, no kiss. Jim rubbed his hands together and said 'right I think I deserve a pint now.' We headed back in the car in silence. I just gazed out the window twisting the ring on my finger, choking back the tears, thinking 'Is that really it, am I really married now?' My heart was totally breaking at the thought of what I had just done and what lay ahead for me in the future. I glanced over at Jim driving and felt nothing.

When we arrived home the house was busy, with people rushing around with plates of food, and more sandwiches and cakes than you can imagine. They all stopped for a moment to congratulate us with beaming smiles. My mother came over and hurriedly asked 'so you did it then?' I nodded and she said 'good', then she just walked off. My stepfather didn't say a word, he was busy charming all the women there with his witty words and willingness to please and help. Jim had gone straight to the makeshift bar that had been set up and poured himself a pint gulping it down as if it were his last drink ever.

I was ushered back upstairs to get ready for the blessing. Mrs Murphy helped me with my dress, putting pins here, there and everywhere to try and make this horrible dress fit me a bit better. Once dressed, my mother and stepfather came into the room, my stepfather was to walk me down the stairs and into the living room where everyone was gathered, everyone belonging to Jim, family and friends – there was no one belonging to me, only my sisters.

As I got ready I turned to my mother and stepfather and started to cry. I told them I didn't want to do it. I begged them to go downstairs and tell everyone I couldn't do it. My stepfather started to laugh and told me not to be so stupid. My mother faced right up to me and told me it was too late, I was already married, the blessing was just for show. She said 'anyway we already got the money.' I asked her what money. Sneering, she told me that Jim had given them money so he could marry me, that's why they signed the consent form. Tears rolled down my face and I felt someone was squeezing my heart. Trying hard not to cry I quietly said 'so you sold me?' My mother wouldn't answer me – she grabbed my arm and told me to stop whinging and to get down those stairs and to stop being a drama queen.

She stormed out of the room and went downstairs leaving

me alone with my stepfather. I sat on the bed trying to control my tears, and for the first time ever my stepfather was kind to me. He sat on the bed next to me and put his arm around me and told me to dry my tears, handing me a tissue. I said to him 'Daddy I really don't want to do this.' He told me it was too late, all I had to do was go downstairs and smile, he told me everything would be okay. A voice came up the stairs saying they were ready for me. My stepfather told me to take a deep breath. As we headed down the stairs I thought my legs would give way, I was shaking from head to toe. We walked into the sitting room through a sea of smiling people and I was presented to Jim. I looked at him and felt sick with fear. The more I saw him that day, the less I wanted to be with him. We went through the motions of the blessing, which was all very religious and formal.

When the ceremony was over Jim headed straight back to the bar, I looked around at all the people chatting and laughing and felt I wanted to run, I wanted to run as fast and as far away as I could from everyone.

I wandered around the house engaging in small talk with some people, but most of the people there were much older than me and I had little or nothing in common with them. I saw the other children playing on the tyre swing outside the kitchen window and longed to be outside with them, they seemed to be having a lot more fun than I was.

That evening Jim and I headed to Dublin and spent our first night as a married couple in a hotel at Dublin airport. We were flying to London for our honeymoon. I asked Jim if he had given my mother money so we could get married, but he just laughed and told me not to be ridiculous. I persisted in questioning him, but he refused to talk about it, he told me none of that mattered now, I was going to have a good life on the farm, away from the slums of Dublin. I would ask him several times over the years I was with him, but I never got a straight answer. It was always the same – 'I took you out of the slums of Dublin and gave you all this, what more do you want?'

We stayed in a hotel in central London, and having never been on a plane before, or even stepped out of Ireland, I looked upon this as a huge adventure. Being in London showed me a whole new world. I had never seen so many people in all my life, straight away I fell in love with the buzz and energy of the city.

Our honeymoon wasn't as I imagined or heard people talk about or had seen on the TV. Jim preferred to spend most of his time in the pub, but we did get to see some of London. I especially remember going to Carnaby Street. I thought I had died and gone to heaven, I loved it! All the shops, all the people dressed like I had never seen before, with Mohican hair styles, piercings to their nose, eyebrows, lips – everyone seemed so happy and carefree. I was just fascinated and decided there and then I loved people watching.

I managed to buy what I thought was a beautiful salmon pink skirt, with a white petticoat underneath held delicately on one side with a little pink bow, along with a white gypsy-style blouse and a pair of red winklepicker shoes. When I tried it all on I felt great, I felt like one of the Londoners I had passed in the street. I couldn't wait to get an opportunity to wear my new outfit. I wore it that very night when Jim and I went for dinner, not that he noticed, but I didn't care, I felt great and for that time that was all that mattered.

Chapter 6

Married Life

When we arrived back on the farm I wasn't sure if I was happy to be there or not, somehow it didn't hold the same excitement for me, and the reality of what was ahead hit me hard. As we went into the house it seemed enormous and empty, and the love I'd had for it before had now turned into fear. Jim dropped our battered suitcase in the hall and said he had to go out.

Suddenly I was left in the huge house all by myself. Tears started to well as I looked around the hallway, the silence was deafening. I walked upstairs to what was to be our bedroom and I started to sob. I felt very trapped. As I looked at the huge windows I saw cobwebs hanging like net curtains covered in dead flies and bluebottles. It was a fabulous house, but it was a working farmhouse and attention to fine details of cleaning were never really considered. As I looked around I couldn't stop crying, but frightened at the prospect of what would be expected of me. One thing I did know was I could not live in a dirty house.

I unpacked the suitcase and started the big clean up. Mrs Rodgers would get cross with me for cleaning and looking back I can understand why – having a teenager around the house cleaning at a hundred miles an hour must have been very difficult for her. I wanted to prove that I was a good wife and I worked very hard cleaning and cooking. I would spend most of my time working in the house.

About a month after we returned from London, I begged Jim to get me a dog. I was so lonely in the big house. We went to a nearby farm and I chose a beautiful black Labrador puppy who I named Rusty. He was great company. I was too young to socialise with the other married women, and Jim didn't want me to be friends with the girls my own age in case they influenced me in any way, so Rusty was the only friend I had. When I did get a bit of free time I would take my guitar and Rusty up to what was known as the High Field. I would sit on a rock and play my guitar and sing at the top of my voice, while Rusty ran around being the mad puppy he was – I adored him.

Life in the big house was very mundane for a teenager. I found it hard living with Jim's mother and father, although they were really lovely people, being together all the time with such a generation gap did become difficult. We decided to get a mobile home to live in and put it in the yard. I was delighted, for me it was like having my own little house and I kept it as spick and span as I could. But I did get very lonely – if Jim wasn't doing as little work as he could, he spent most of his time in the pub.

I longed for the holidays when my sisters or my two old school friends would come to visit. We would have great fun, we would take the caravan cushions out on to the grass tennis court, line them all up to make what was one big mat and do gymnastics. Jim would get very cross if he caught me doing that. I remember him marching up from the field several times and shouting at me saying I was making a fool of him and that no

CHAPTER 6: MARRIED LIFE

wife of his should still be playing. I couldn't understand what I had done so wrong, but Jim didn't want me to have much to do with any of my friends. Even though I was married, I so longed to do what all 16 and 17 year olds were doing – having sleepovers, going to dances, talking about hair and makeup and boys.

When I turned 17 I decided I wanted to go back to school and do my Leaving Certificate so I could get some qualifications and possibly get a good job. I applied to a high school in the local town and much to my delight I was called for an interview with the headmaster. I might have been married, but I was still so scared when I was presented to the headmaster. I explained to him that I had left school when I was 15 and now realised that I did want to finish my education. He told me that he would be happy to accept me in his school, but just because I was married there would be no special allowances for me – I would like all the other children, have to wear a uniform and attend all classes. I agreed and was so delighted and excited that I was to have a second chance.

When I got home, I couldn't wait to tell Jim, so as soon as I saw him I just blurted it out. I excitedly told him what the headteacher had said about the rules and regulations, but before I had a chance to say anything else Jim got so mad. He started to shout at me, saying I was making a fool of him, he said there was no way that any wife of his was going back to school and make him a laughing stock. As he was shouting at me I had that horrid feeling like your heart is being squashed, I could feel tears well in my eyes as he continued to shout at me, but if you asked me what else he'd said I couldn't have told you, I switched off at the words 'no way are you going'. I had the humiliation of having to ring the headmaster with some silly excuse as to why I couldn't attend. I was devastated. Jim was very happy and life just went on.

To keep busy I started to get involved with village life, helping to get the tennis courts up and running again. I got involved in amateur dramatics which I enjoyed, but my biggest love was the music group. Myself and a local woman got together and decided to start a women's folk group – we had four guitarists including myself, and about eight other singers. I loved the rehearsals and performing. I was at my happiest playing my guitar and singing for all I was worth. We mainly played gospel songs, which went down very well at Mass on Sundays. I did raise a few whispers though, being married to a Protestant and singing in a Catholic church did cause a bit of a stir, but I didn't care, I just wanted to play my guitar and sing. I decided to try to keep everyone happy I would go to the 10 a.m. Protestant church service, then I would run down to the other end of the village to make the 11 a.m. Mass with the other members of the folk group. We became quite good, and were asked on several occasions to play at funerals and special Mass services.

When I was 19 I found out I was pregnant. I was delighted, I really wanted a baby, a little person I could show just how much love I had to give. Here I was now, my prayers had been answered, I was going to have a beautiful little baby.

My pregnancy was very hard, I had a lot of illness throughout, and being a romantic sentimental fool, I decided that I wanted my baby to be born in the same hospital that I was born in. I would have to make my way up to Dublin by bus which wasn't very nice especially when I was nearing my birth time. Jim wouldn't take me in the car.

CHAPTER 6: MARRIED LIFE

My mother was still being a pain, constantly ringing wanting something or another. When I was seven months pregnant and really unwell, my mother decided to send my sister Patricia down to stay with me, not to look after me or help me, but rather the other way around. Patricia had suffered a nervous breakdown and my mother did not want the responsibility of looking after her. I didn't mind so much as it was nice to have the company, even though she cried constantly, but she never told me until a few years later as to why she'd had a nervous breakdown.

One night while Patricia was staying, I was feeling very unwell so I decided to go to bed early. I remember Jim coming to bed at some stage, then I woke later in the night to find he was gone. I got up to look for him and for some reason decided to look in the room where my sister was sleeping. I nearly died when I found Jim in bed trying to have sex with her, my sister was only 17. I was in shock, Jim quickly jumped up and ran out after me, but my sister never moved. I was totally distraught. I asked him what did he think he was doing? And straight away he blamed me saying that it was my fault, because I was pregnant he didn't like me that way, he tried to tell me I didn't understand him. I remember feeling physically sick at what he had just done. I didn't know what to do, again, believing that it was my fault, I became afraid, I worried what his mother and father would say, he begged me not to tell them to which I stupidly agreed.

The next day was our wedding anniversary. Jim was fussing around me like an old hen, but any time I looked at him I hated him even more. I tried to talk to my sister about what happened, but she didn't want to know – she said she didn't remember anything because of the heavy medication she was taking. So once again I withdrew and became insular, totally believing that everything was my fault. I tried to mend my broken heart by crocheting some dressing table mats for my mother, I know it sounds a strange thing to do, but I really didn't know what else to do. I also stupidly believed that when my baby was born, this would fix everything. How silly a girl can be.

I went into labour in the spring of 1986. When I started to get the really bad pains it took me back to that day in Ballymun when I was sent home from work. Stephanie was born in May 1986, a gorgeous little girl with the biggest blue eyes you can imagine. I was in total awe of this beautiful bundle, as I looked at her though the glass cot she was placed in beside me minutes after she was born, I was fascinated at how perfect she was and how her blue eyes were trying to scan all around her. Like any mother with their child, I cannot explain the deep true love I had for my beautiful daughter, for me it was an experience of love I had never had before. I didn't want to put Stephanie down for one second, I just wanted to hold her, smell her, love her. The nurses would come in to me several times and tell me I had to put her down, or she would expect to be held all the time. I hated having to put her in the crib, and I hated even more when the nurses would come and take all the babies away after the 10 p.m. feed. I would lie in bed worried that she was missing me, or that when the nurses brought her back to me in the morning I would get the wrong baby. Silly I know, but I couldn't help feeling that way.

When we were finally allowed home, I was delighted to show Stephanie the little nursery I had created for her while I was pregnant. I had also knitted some cardigans for her, in neutral

CHAPTER 6: MARRIED LIFE

colours because I didn't know if I was going to have a boy or a girl. Now this baby I had spoken of all the time was really here, and I was just so in love.

When we arrived at the house Rusty ran up as always to greet me, he jumped up while I had Stephanie in my arms and was very keen to investigate this bundle I was holding. He didn't do anything bad, only get a little over-excited. Jim was furious, he grabbed Rusty and punched him in the face, sending him yelping down the farmyard. I was so mad with him for doing that. But with all the excitement of bringing Stephanie home and showing her off to her grandparents, I completely forgot about Rusty that day.

It wasn't until that evening when Stephanie was having a cuddle with her grandma that I decided to go and feed Rusty. I went outside and called him. It was very unusual that he wouldn't zoom around the corner as soon as he heard my voice, but this evening no matter how many times I called he didn't come. I was worried, but decided that he was still hiding from Jim, and would probably come back later. I went back indoors and got into a conversation with Mrs Rodgers as to who Stephanie looked like, it was decided after going through the family that Stephanie did actually look like me, much to my delight. Mr Rodgers did not have too much to say, only to tell me his disappointment that Stephanie was a girl, he wanted a grandson to take over the farm, a granddaughter was not what he wanted. I felt a little hurt and again a failure at what he said, but looking at Stephanie I was delighted that she was a girl. I swore when I was holding her that no man would ever hurt her as I had been hurt.

When I went to bed that first night I put her in a little carry cot that I had beside the bed, and she lay there wide awake just looking around her as she had done in the hospital. I couldn't stop looking at her and held her hand as I watched her gently fall asleep. Jim finally came to bed, he had been out most of the day. I remembered Rusty, so I asked Jim if he'd fed him, but he started to snigger and took great delight in telling me he had gotten rid of Rusty. My heart dropped when I asked him what he meant, he told me that Rusty was jealous of Stephanie and it would only be a matter of time before he would have hurt her, so he had decided to have him put down. As he was coldly telling me this I could feel my heart squeezing again – how could he do that to my dog, my beloved Rusty? I tried very hard not to cry, and to think positively that although Rusty was gone, I had a beautiful baby to look after now.

Life with Stephanie was a little hard in that she cried a lot – she had bad colic that seemed to go on for hours, days, nights, weeks and even months. Her constant crying put an even bigger strain on what was already a desperately unhappy marriage. I loved Stephanie so much and no matter how I tried to help her I couldn't get rid of her colic. Then one day I heard that goats' milk was very good for colic. I found a farmer on the other side of the village who kept goats for milking, so I used to go every other day to his farm to get a carton of goats' milk.

Shortly after starting Stephanie on the milk she became so much better and once she started walking she was fine. I was now enjoying motherhood so much and coping better than I had done when she was first born. She was like a little doll to me, I loved to dress her up and put bows and ribbons in her wispy black hair. I wrote a song for Stephanie thanking God for giving her to me.

CHAPTER 6: MARRIED LIFE

> A gift so wonderful and free
> A gift that Jesus gave to me
> A child to bear, to love and rear.
> Jesus answered my prayer
> He looked down with loving eyes,
> He blessed me with a beautiful child
> Jesus answered my prayer.

I was just so in love with her, and truly wanted to thank God for giving me such a beautiful little girl.

Things between Jim and I went from bad to worse, we hardly communicated at all, and he was spending more and more time in the pub with little or no regard for Stephanie and me. But we were fine, I had built up a nice circle of friends who had babies of a similar age to Stephanie so she was quite contented.

Chapter 7

Allegations

Stephanie was just over a year old when I was hit with another bombshell. My stepfather and mother arrived unexpectedly with my youngest half-sister Sheila. My mother was in tears and very shaken, she blurted out that they had just come from the police station in Tallaght, where my stepfather had been interviewed at length over sexual abuse allegations made by my half-sister Catherine. I stood frozen to the spot, feeling I had been punched in the stomach. I wanted to scream 'its true!' but I couldn't speak. My stepfather told my mother to go for a walk and calm down, it was disgusting to watch as he gave her a hug and played the victim with an Oscar-winning performance.

My poor sister, in a home, abandoned, called a liar – I can't tell you what was going through my head. I only know that I was terrified, even more so now he had me on his own. He calmly put on the Voice, the one that scared me when he wanted something, I felt weak at the knees and sick like I was going to pass out, like I could die on the spot at that very moment. He told me that he was in a lot of trouble and that he could go to prison, he grabbed me by the throat and held me up against the wall and in no uncertain terms told me that if I were to breathe a word he would kill my baby, my mother and Sheila, and then

CHAPTER 7: ALLEGATIONS

kill himself. He said, 'Now, would you want all that on your shoulders? Would you want to be the one to blame for all this?'

I was frozen with fear, and went from being a fairly confident young woman to being a small helpless little girl again. He took his hand off my throat and lit a cigarette and told me he had also warned Sharon and Patricia, that he would kill them too if they said a word.

I felt I had been hit by a train when he said that. Oh my God! Was he saying he abused them too? Oh my God! That is exactly what he was saying! I wanted to run, I wanted to be sick, I wanted to scream, I wanted to die, I wanted to do I don't know what. I couldn't breathe properly, it was like my throat was closing with shock. My mother reappeared before I had time to think, she was still crying and shaking, she looked like a child herself that day, she looked broken and vulnerable.

My mother said 'What do you think of that bitch Catherine saying all that about your poor dad?' I stood there screaming inside, 'Oh my God! Please don't tell me you believe him! Please do not stand there and pretend you did not know what was going on.'

I could not believe that her tears were for herself and the animal she had married, I thought her tears were for her daughter, my sister, but how silly was I to think that? She had only ever thought of herself and him so why should I have expected anything different. She told me Catherine had been taken into care because she was difficult – Catherine was not difficult, she was a beautiful child, a quite timid little child. I was in so much shock I didn't know how to react, all I could think was he was going to kill my baby, but how could I defend him against my little sister? Oh my God what was I going to do?

My mother was going on and on about Catherine, saying how nasty she was, she called her spawn of Satan. I was sick with fear, panic and anger. I had a pain in my heart like never before, how could my mother talk with such contempt for my little sister Catherine, how could she put her in care? How could she be so selfish and live in such denial of what he had done? Not content with ruining my life, he had done it to his own flesh and blood, his own daughters, all three of them. My mother sitting in the kitchen sobbing, continued with her barrage of nastiness towards Catherine, my stepfather sat holding her hand. Sat before me were two very evil people, and they happened to be my parents.

My mother ranted and raved about how social services would take Sheila if Catherine did not stop all the lies and accusations. She looked me straight in the eye and said to me, 'I know that it's all lies, your Daddy never touched her, it's all lies isn't it Cassie?' I couldn't answer, I wanted to, I wanted to say 'No! It's not lies! It's all true, every single word is true, the man sat beside you is an animal, he is not fit to be called a man, he has raped all your children.' I opened my mouth but nothing came out. I just looked at the floor.

At that moment Jim came into the room carrying Stephanie. My stepfather jumped up and asked Jim if he could hold her, Jim willingly handed my baby over to him, I froze. As he brushed his hairy beard along her soft beautiful skin and planted a kiss on her cheek, he glanced over at me and smiled a sinister smile. I felt sick, he was breathing all over her, my knees were like jelly. Stephanie started to cry, so I quickly took her out of his arms and cuddled her so tight into my chest. My stepfather said 'even my own granddaughter doesn't like me', but my

CHAPTER 7: ALLEGATIONS

mother jumped up and flung her arms around him, still crying saying 'Christy, don't say that, we all love you, don't we Cassie?' I didn't say a word.

My mother continued to rip Catherine apart and told me that we all had to go to Dublin to be interviewed by social services, she told me that they wanted to see Sheila on her own and do some games with her to find out if she was being abused. I was listening to all this, trying to take it all in, the more they talked about it, the more frightened I felt, the tighter I held on to Stephanie. I could see that Jim was drawing my mother out, getting her to talk more and more about it, almost as if he was thriving on it. My stepfather sat looking all forlorn, loving the fact that both my mother and Jim were piling sympathy on him. But what about poor Catherine? What was she going through? What was I to do? If I told the truth, my stepfather would kill my baby – if I lied and said it wasn't true then I would be letting Catherine down and denying the pain that she was going through and my own pain. My head was so messed up I couldn't think straight. When my mother and stepfather finally left, I thought my head would surely burst.

The day came for the meeting with social services in Dublin. Sharon, Patricia and myself managed to get a few minutes alone outside, Patricia was shaking from head to toe, Sharon didn't say too much, the three of us were so uncomfortable, none of us knew what to say. Patricia started to get very upset, she said that she couldn't go through all this, she said that we had to lie or Daddy was going to kill us all. I looked at my sisters and saw that they were every bit as broken as I was and I thought about my baby. I felt sick at the thought of anything happening to her. We made the decision to say that the abuse allegations were not true, a decision we were all to regret for the rest of our lives and a decision that was to destroy our bond as sisters.

The hearing was set for a day in June 1987. It was my stepfather's birthday, and during the course of the interview when questions got too much for him, he would burst into tears and say 'this is no way to spend my birthday.' We were all brought into a room with a two-way mirror. My mother, stepfather, me, Jim, Sharon, Patricia and Sheila with a few people from social services present, we were sat in a circle as the questions went on for what seemed like hours. There was no sign of Catherine, we were not allowed to see her, we were only told that she had made these accusations and that she was very upset. The question was asked to my stepfather, why would she make such an allegation? My mother piped up it was because she was evil, sent from the devil.

Both my mother and stepfather spoke of their true faith in God, telling that they were born again Christians and that to suggest such a thing was wrong. They both spoke with such denial and gave such an outstanding performance that even I thought, is it true? Did I dream it all?

The questioning of my sisters and I was so hard – to have to sit there and lie knowing that the man and woman who took my childhood away were sitting across the room from me, totally believing that they were innocent. I couldn't look at my sisters, I couldn't look at anyone, I kept my eyes focused on the floor. I could feel my stepfather's glare, and the fear I felt from his stare made me feel like a child again. One by one we all denied the abuse. It was one of the most horrible things I have ever done, to lie to protect such an animal, but I didn't do it to protect him. I did it through fear, pure fear at the thought of

CHAPTER 7: ALLEGATIONS

losing my baby, and seeing my mother and sisters killed. I had no reason to doubt that my stepfather would not carry out his threat, nor could I take the chance.

We left the social services offices exhausted, none of us girls talking, our heads held low as each of us dealt with our own thoughts. My mother and stepfather were hugging each other and crying, truly believing that they had been vindicated, but it was not to end there, in fact it was to get a lot worse.

Sharon and Patricia went back to their lives, both were working and living in Dublin. I went back to the farm and tried to piece my life back together, but us sisters never had the same relationship again after that, and when we did see each other it was all very strained. Sharon became very insular almost with an air of arrogance; Patricia was running on nervous energy, she would talk at a hundred miles an hour about anything and everything, but never about what had happened; Catherine, when she started her own life, went off the rails for a while. We did all get together and stayed in touch for a few years, but the trauma of the abuse drove a wedge between us and after a while we lost contact.

After that day of the hearing I threw myself into being the best mum and housewife I could be. I became more and more involved in the ladies' folk group and got involved with as much as I could in the village. I would dress like I was a city slicker and walk with my head held high, smiling and chatting to all I encountered. I tried to hide the shame I was carrying by being as busy as I possibly could, if I am honest I probably had an air of superiority about me, but I looked and behaved like I was fully in control of everything in my life, when in actual fact I was dying inside.

I had terrible nightmares after that day in Dublin. Every single day I thought of the lie I had told, I thought of my poor sister and how I had let her down. When I closed my eyes I would see Catherine's little face and I would feel such pain inside for what I had done. I would pray every day that God would forgive me. I would look at Stephanie and hug her all the time. I was now as bad as my mother and stepfather, I too was living in denial.

Jim would ask me questions about my childhood, but I tried not to tell him too much. I wanted to try and forget all about it, but he wouldn't let it go. He would smile as he asked almost like he got a kick out of hearing what I had to say about my childhood. He would ask me intimate questions about my stepfather which I would refuse to answer – I would pretend I couldn't hear him, and I would never let him know that he had upset me. He would remind me regularly of my poverty-stricken background and would let me know that I should feel privileged that I was living with him now, that he was some sort of hero for taking me away from all that hardship. Little did he know just how much I had come to dislike him.

Just weeks before Christmas 1987 the abuse case against my stepfather was still continuing – even though my sisters and I had denied anything had gone on, the police in Tallaght kept on with their investigation. A police officer called Sergeant O'Shea was in charge of the case and he really believed that my stepfather was lying. He kept the investigation going by having Sheila fully questioned and examined to make sure she had not been abused – it was proved at that time that she had not. Sergeant O'Shea never questioned me, but he did speak to Sharon and Patricia – again, both girls stuck to their story.

CHAPTER 7: ALLEGATIONS

For me at that time things were not great at all. Jim and I were arguing all the time, my mother was constantly on the phone telling me the dreadful stories of what was happening back in Dublin, and I felt trapped and suffocated, living with the lie I'd told, it was eating at me like a disease. I could not stop thinking about Catherine, every day wondering how she was.

Jim decided to do some work in the house, he decided that it was time we had our own space, if we had that, maybe we could make the marriage work. I was less than sure of that, our marriage was really dead in the water by then, but I went along with getting the house done up, it was in need of some TLC. He decided that the house was big enough to divide into two, his mother and father living downstairs, we upstairs. A bathroom was fitted downstairs and a kitchen was fitted upstairs for us. A partition wall with a door was put in the hallway and both parties had their own separate entrances and front doors. It worked well and still left each of us with more than enough rooms to ramble around in. But the new renovations did nothing to enhance or change the way things were in our marriage.

Chapter 8

My Knight in Shining Armour

That Christmas Jim decided he would go to Canada with his mother, leaving me and Stephanie at home. I was upset I wasn't going too, as Canada was a place I would have loved to have gone, but not necessarily with Jim. But when I thought about it I was kind of glad he was going, at least I wouldn't have to spend Christmas with him. He went for three weeks over the holidays, leaving me with very little money, but I didn't care, I was just happy to have peace and quiet, and I was determined to give Stephanie a good Christmas. Because I didn't have a lot of money I couldn't afford an expensive present for her, so I went to a jumble sale and found a lovely doll's cradle, it was a little worse for wear but I could see it could be really lovely. I got a friend from the village to fix it up and paint it for me and I have to say when I got it back it looked brand new. I made some little bed linen for it and had enough money to buy a little doll to fit inside. On Christmas morning, I got so much joy from seeing the delight on Stephanie's face, we had a quiet but lovely day and Jim's sister was there with her children.

Jim didn't ring often while he was away, but when he did ring we had nothing to say to each other so we would argue. Having time away from him made me realise that I truly didn't love him,

CHAPTER 8: MY KNIGHT IN SHINING ARMOUR

it gave me a very sad feeling because I felt trapped, I was just 21 years old and desperately unhappy. This was not what I had planned for my life all those years ago.

Then that very Christmas I met someone who was to have a huge impact on my life for the next 25 years. Some friends I had made from the village who were nearer my age, called up to see Stephanie and I, and they invited me to a party that was being held in town. I was reluctant to go, because I had no money and no one to look after Stephanie, so I said I wouldn't bother going. However, they had organised a babysitter for me as a surprise and told me not to worry about money. I felt excited about going out, I hadn't been out for ages. So I put on my gladrags, did my hair and make-up and headed out to the party. It felt great to laugh and joke like the young woman I was. I loved that feeling of freedom, doing what I should be doing at my age.

When we arrived at the party, there was a band playing, but at first I didn't take much notice of them because I was so excited and nervous meeting all the family of my friends. I got myself a drink and settled down to enjoy myself. I looked over at the band playing and noticed the bass player, a very handsome sexy man as I thought, with thick jet-black hair, tight jeans and open-necked shirt. There was something very attractive about him, he really had the rock star look.

As the evening went on, my friends and I danced until our legs hurt. I was having the time of my life and I noticed that the bass player wouldn't take his eyes off me. He was singing love songs and looking straight at me, I felt he was singing directly to me – I was so flattered by his attention. I asked my friend who he was and she told me he was her uncle Damien.

For the rest of the evening Damien and I made flirtatious eye contact. I was having a wonderful time.

When the band was packing up at the end of the night, Damien came over to talk to me – he had the most amazing soft English accent, a beautiful smile and lovely eyes. I thought he was the most gorgeous man I had ever seen, we chatted for a while mainly about music, I felt really nervous and awkward with him and was sure I was making a fool of myself. When it was time to leave Damien asked if he could see me again, I told him I was married and had a little girl, but I knew deep inside that I really wanted to see him again. We exchanged phone numbers. I went home feeling like I was walking on air. For the first time in ages I felt really happy and excited.

The next day Damien called me and we laughed and chatted on the phone for ages. He asked to see me that day, which I agreed to without any hesitation, and within an hour he was sitting in my front room, looking more gorgeous than I had remembered from the night before. I was becoming totally besotted by him. Damien was almost 18 years older than me and at the time that made him even more attractive to me. I was in total awe of him, as he told me stories of the many rock stars he had met through his life in rock and roll London of the 60s and 70s.

I was having feelings that I had not experienced before. I just wanted to talk and talk to him, he was very attentive and actually seemed interested in me and what I had to say, no one had done that before, and he was everything that Jim wasn't. I put Stephanie to bed, then we chatted some more. He had brought a bottle of white wine with him and to me that was the ultimate statement of sophistication. As we chatted and giggled

CHAPTER 8: MY KNIGHT IN SHINING ARMOUR

together, Damien leaned in and kissed me, I had never been kissed like that before nor had I felt like I felt before. I believe I fell in love with him there and then.

Our relationship developed from that moment on and we became almost inseparable. For the next ten days we saw each other every single day, and everywhere we went we took Stephanie with us. We were having a ball, I couldn't have been any happier at that time. We spoke about being together permanently and for me that seemed almost like a dream. I was in love with Damien and he with me: it made perfect sense for us to be together. So we sat one evening and planned our future together. I said I wanted to go to London, I wanted to be as far away from my mother and stepfather as possible, and as I had been to London before and loved it, and Damien had spent almost 25 years in London, it made perfect sense for us to start our new lives there.

Then Jim came back from Canada and the reality of my life kicked in. How could I leave him? I mean it was almost unheard of in Ireland for a woman to walk out and leave her husband. When Jim came back things were very bad between us, but now mainly caused by me. I couldn't bear to be in the same room as him any more. I was in love with Damien and I just wanted to be with him.

So about three weeks into my relationship with Damien, I sat Jim down and told him I didn't love him any more. I told him I was leaving and heading to London, needless to say Jim didn't take it too well, he was very upset and begged me to stay. I told him I couldn't stay, my mind was made up and I was going. We had a long discussion about Stephanie, I said I was taking her with me, he said I couldn't, he said Ireland was her home, she had her grandparents and all she knew around her, if I was going to London where was I taking her to? I told him I would work it all out, but I was definitely taking my baby with me. We ended up having a big fight about it, I dug my heels in and insisted that Stephanie was coming with me.

The next few days were very stressful, Mr and Mrs Rodgers were very upset at the news I was leaving. The atmosphere in the house for those few days was terrible. I felt a huge sense of guilt for what I was doing, but also a sense of excitement at the prospect of a brand new life in London, free from abuse, free from unhappiness, just a feeling of pure freedom.

Two days before I was due to leave, Jim asked me where I would be staying when I got to London. I told him I would be staying with friends in a place in north London, I told him I had planned to then get a job and a place to live. This is what Damien and I had discussed. Jim argued that he felt this was not the right situation to take Stephanie to. He felt it would be better if I were to go to London first and get a job and somewhere to live, then he said he would be happier letting Stephanie come to me.

I was devastated, was he trying to take my baby? I couldn't let him do that. I tried to convince him that everything would be okay and he had nothing to worry about, I told him I was Stephanie's mother and I would take very good care of her. I was dreadfully upset and couldn't bear the thought of leaving her behind, it was an unthinkable idea. Jim told me I would be irresponsible to take a child to a country I had never lived in without a proper home to offer her. He promised me that if I got a job and provided a home for Stephanie he would have no hesitation in letting her come to me. I had a train running

CHAPTER 8: MY KNIGHT IN SHINING ARMOUR

through my head, I couldn't go and leave Stephanie, she was the most precious person in my life, she was my baby.

I went to see Damien and told him what Jim had said, he told me I had to take her, I had to try and get her out of the house and bring her with me. The day before I was going to London was pure hell. I was in a terrible state – Jim was putting so much pressure on me not to go, Mrs Rodgers was begging me not to take Stephanie, but I stood firm and told them all I was going and I was taking Stephanie with me.

The night before I was due to leave I packed up most of Stephanie's things. Jim had gone to the pub and I felt a little of the pressure was off me, but I was still in a dreadful state. I dared not tell my mother I was going because I knew that she would come straight down to stop me. I couldn't tell anyone what I was doing. I put Stephanie to bed that night hugging and kissing her, telling her how much I loved her, and promising her that I would give her the best life I could when we got to London. I walked around the house that night looking at the rooms that had been my home for five years, feeling empty and like I had just seen them for the first time, I felt nothing. I climbed into bed and had a very restless night. I heard Jim come home from the pub and slam shut his bedroom door.

The next morning when I woke, I felt excited and nervous at the new life that lay ahead. I went into Stephanie's room to get her up, thinking it was strange that she hadn't called me as she did every morning. Each morning when she woke, she would call 'Ma, ma', and I would go and get her, sometimes bringing her in to my bed for a cuddle, but this morning she didn't call me. I walked into her room and she was not there. I felt sick, I ran around calling her but there was no sound. I went into Jim's bedroom but he wasn't there either. I was in a blind panic. I ran downstairs calling Stephanie and Jim, but no answer came. I tried to open the partition door in the hallway but it was locked. I knocked and knocked on the door, I could hear Stephanie on the other side, Jim came to the door and opened it, I told him I wanted Stephanie, he said 'no way'. I was almost hysterical as I begged him to give me back my baby, but he just laughed at me and said that I was not going to see Stephanie again that day. He told me I could have her and see her when I was settled in London as agreed, but under no circumstances would I see her today.

I was distraught. Mrs Rodgers walked by Jim with Stephanie in her arms, I tried to push past him to get to Stephanie as she was calling 'ma, ma', but he pushed me back, grabbed the door and locked it again. I was totally hysterical, I didn't know what to do. I felt my heart was being ripped out of me, as I heard Stephanie cry out for me. I sat on the floor by the door and sobbed for what seemed like ages, begging and begging for my baby back, but they wouldn't answer me or let me see her. Almost on my knees I went shaking back upstairs and rang Damien. I told him what Jim had done, he told me to dry my tears and be strong, he told me not to worry, that when we got to London he would make sure I got Stephanie back. He seemed to think that Jim would stick to his word and let Stephanie come over when we were sorted.

I dried my tears and tried to convince myself that everything would be okay. Damien and I had agreed to meet at Dublin airport in the early evening. As I was putting the last few bits of mine together, I heard the partition door open. I ran downstairs to see if I could get to Stephanie, but Jim had come through to

CHAPTER 8: MY KNIGHT IN SHINING ARMOUR

our side and locked the door again. I became hysterical, I begged and begged him to let me have my baby, he just grabbed my arms squeezing them tight and shouted at me, that there was no way I was taking her today, that he had agreed to let her go when I had somewhere to live. He told me to calm down, that he had something he wanted to say me.

We went into our kitchen upstairs, he reached in his pocket and took out a cheque for £10,000 and told me that this money was in full and final settlement of any claim I could make on his property. I was in such a state I couldn't quite take in what was happening. I had never asked him for money, nor had I any intention of taking his farm, I didn't understand about things like that, I didn't know that I could be entitled to half of all he had and to be honest, I didn't care about all that, I just wanted my baby back.

When he put that cheque in my hand I got a glimmer of hope. I told him that now I had money I could go straight away and get a flat, so there was no need for Stephanie to stay, I could take her with me now. Jim said no way, a deal was a deal, but I hadn't agreed to anything. He firmly told me that I could have Stephanie once I was settled and that was that. He turned on his heels to walk out, then stopped and told me there was no need for me to get the bus to Dublin, he would take me.

I stood there snivelling like a child, desperately frightened and desperately wanting to hold my baby. Not sure what to do. Maybe I should stay, maybe things would get better between Jim and me, maybe I could learn to like him. Somehow the thought of spending the rest of my life there scared the life out of me, I just knew I had to go. As I carried my two suitcases down the stairs, Jim was standing waiting for me. I dropped the suitcases on the floor and begged him to let me see Stephanie, he told me to wait by the front door. He was gone for what seemed like ages, then through the partition door came Jim with his mother who was carrying my baby. I ran to Stephanie and put my arms out to hold her, but Mrs Rodgers pulled her away, Jim said I could say goodbye to her from there, I was not to hold her. Stephanie put her arms out to me and was calling 'ma ma, ma ma'. I was absolutely sobbing, I begged them to let me hold her but they wouldn't, I kissed her and kissed her not wanting to stop, but his mother pulled her away and walked back through the door. I tried to run after her, but Jim pulled me back. Stephanie had her hand out, she was crying, 'ma ma, ma ma'. I thought I was going to die on the spot of a broken heart.

    I got into the car and all I could see and hear was Stephanie's face and her voice calling me. I thought I would stop breathing as we drove away from the house. Jim told me to stop crying, as it was only a temporary situation and that I was getting myself into a state for nothing. As we drove out of the village, Jim didn't take the turn for Dublin, but he said he wanted to take me to his solicitor to sign a piece of paper to say that I would not take any of his farm from him. Still not understanding the implications, I wholeheartedly agreed. When we got to the solicitor's office, I was still in a state, the solicitor was talking to me about the letter I had to sign, but it wasn't a letter, there was quite a number of pages. As he was talking to me I couldn't hear a word he was saying, I was still feeling numb from leaving Stephanie. Jim told him I had to catch a plane so we needed to hurry. I was given the same pages to sign twice, one copy for me and the other for Jim. I didn't even look at the papers, I just signed them, with no emotion or questions.

CHAPTER 8: MY KNIGHT IN SHINING ARMOUR

Jim and I got back in the car and headed to Dublin. It was a horrible silent journey, my mind was very noisy though, I was thinking that I was so determined to make a good life in London with Damien, and I would most definitely get my daughter back. I was busy making plans and imagining how our lives would be, and now I didn't feel so heartbroken with those lovely thoughts. We pulled into the airport and I said a very cold goodbye to Jim, I shook his hand and said 'see you around.' As I walked away, Jim called after me that I was a stupid bitch, he started to laugh and told me he wouldn't see me around, and to make sure I had a good look at what I had signed. Still not understanding I looked at him and said 'I know what I signed, I didn't want any of your stupid farm anyway.'

I turned again and kept walking, I checked in, and went to meet Damien in the bar. When I saw him I was both relieved and tearful. We didn't get much time before our flight was called, but once we had taken off Damien ordered champagne. I had never had champagne before in my life, I was so excited, I really believed that this was the way life would be when I got to London. As we were chatting Damien asked me why I was a bit late, he joked that he thought I wasn't going to show up. I took out the papers I signed and showed them to him, naively babbling on about how Jim had made me do a detour to his solicitor's to sign these stupid papers.

Damien flicked through them, and stopped at one of the clauses, which said that I waived all rights of the custody of Stephanie, that I consented to Jim having full custody and control over my daughter. I felt I had been stabbed in the heart, as the words jumped off the page. Did I just sign my daughter away? Had I really been that stupid? Yes I did, and yes I was.

Damien told me not to worry, he knew solicitors in London who would get my daughter back, he reassured me in such a way that I, for the first time that day, felt a calmness inside.

When we arrived in London, it was dark and quite late. Damien's brother had come to meet us and we were to stay with him and his girlfriend until we got a place of our own. As we were driving through London I felt overwhelmed. There was so much traffic and so many people, I had never noticed it when I was in London before. I wondered where was everyone going at such a late hour.

When we arrived at Damien's brother's apartment, for some reason I felt quite emotional, and I couldn't control the tears. I excused myself and went to the bathroom to pull myself together. I could hear Damien and his brother talking about going out for something to eat – I felt panicked, 'how can we go out at this time? Everywhere will be closed.' I heard Damien's brother suggest we go for Indian food, I had never had Indian food before and was so sure I would not like it. Damien very sweetly told his brother that I would probably prefer Chinese. When we got to the restaurant, Damien's brother ordered all the food, food I had never heard of or seen before, I was just used to sweet and sour pork. Damien could see I was a little freaked out and very quietly and sensitively helped me.

Although I was in love with Damien, my heart was breaking for Stephanie. Every morning I would wake and I was so sure I could hear her call me, I would cry a lot from the pain in my heart for my little girl. Damien reassured me that as soon as we got our own place we would get Stephanie back.

Chapter 9

Doubts

A few days into our stay in north London, Damien's brother's girlfriend asked me out for a drink. We went to a very trendy wine bar, and as we sat there having our drinks, she turned to me and very seriously and frankly told me to be careful of Damien, that he had a history of beating up women. When she said that, I thought I would choke, I had just left my baby and come to England with a man I had only known for three weeks, how stupid was I? What had I done? I thought for a moment – maybe she was lying, maybe she is just trying to cause problems, but at the same time I was terrified, had I just jumped from the frying pan into the fire? I decided to be grown up about the whole thing and confront Damien with what had been said to me. I mean I had no reason to think that Damien would ever hurt me, he was so loving towards me.

When I got home I decided against asking him, I think part of me was afraid of the answer I would receive. So I put it all to the back of my mind and just enjoyed the time I was having with Damien. I was so in love with him and felt so happy and safe in his presence. Every day he would assure me that we would get Stephanie back, and that we would have a great life.

Ten days after arriving in London we moved into our own place. It was a converted garage made into a studio flat in west London, it was a bit cold and damp but I loved it, it was just perfect for the two of us to start our new lives together. We were so happy, I didn't think it was possible to be that happy. We had such lovely times for the first few weeks, but burning away in the back of my mind was what had been said to me in the wine bar. I tried not to think about it too much, but a huge part of me wanted to know. I had suffered so much abuse before and I couldn't bear to suffer any more.

One night while we were out having dinner, I awkwardly brought up what was said to me. When I asked Damien he just laughed and told me not to be ridiculous, he had never hit a woman in his life. As far as I was concerned that was enough for me and we continued to have a lovely time. But it wasn't long until I was to learn the truth.

Damien and I had been living together in London for just a few weeks when I experienced his first jealous outburst. I had got a job working in a bakery, which I really enjoyed. I was making friends and enjoying the experience of working again. Damien would insist on walking me to work every day and walking me home in the evenings even though the shop was just at the end of our road. I thought it was really nice and romantic of him to do that. What I didn't know was that he was consistently jealous and possessive of me. When he collected me from work he would ask me a thousand questions about my day: Who came into the shop? What where they like? What did they say? I didn't at first find it strange, I just thought he was interested in my day, until one particular evening he came to collect me. A couple of builders had come in for sandwiches

CHAPTER 9: DOUBTS

The Black Panther

The Black Panther can sometimes be polite
As he licks his lips from his last bite.
He prowls around you and says kind words
Makes you feel safe in this cruel world.
So you trust him to look after you, he says you'll be safe,
But you know deep inside you need to escape
He says 'its okay, I'm not going to hurt you,
I just want to play.'

He prowls and he prowls, you see a safe place
You want to run.
He sees your fear and laughs 'not yet my precious one.'
He licks his lips and prowls some more
You look past his eyes, you can see the door.
You look in his eyes begging to be free
In his soft voice he says 'trust in me'
You resist his soft voice and beg once more.
Then with a roar he pounces, using you like a whore.

He throws you around like a raw piece of meat,
You lie there helpless feeling defeat.
The Panther strides off slamming the door
As you lay there broken on the kitchen floor.
When will it stop? you scream inside
Where can I go, where can I hide?
You pull yourself up, wipe away your tears
Christ… this abuse has been going on years.
But the cycle continues day after day
You're trapped, you can't run away.

that day and had started some harmless flirtatious banter with myself and the other girls. We were giggling as girls do, and from the corner of my eye I saw Damien with an expression on his face I had never seen before – it made me a little nervous, but I chose to ignore it, I mean this was my boyfriend not my stepfather.

As soon as we were heading home, the questions started again, but this time I could sense that Damien was not happy. When we got indoors I suddenly felt quite nervous, I tried to humour him and make light conversation, but he wasn't having any of it. He started to raise his voice, and twist and turn everything I was saying, accusing me of wanting to be with the builders that had come into the shop. I tried very hard to convince him that we were only chatting, but he wouldn't listen. The next thing I knew he had slapped me across the face sending me flying on to the bed. He was shouting at me that I was making a fool of him. I just lay on the bed frozen in fear, tears streaming down my face, this was the man I loved, how could he do this to me? I was so scared, is this what I had left Ireland for? Is this what I left my baby for? Damien stormed out of our flat slamming the door, I just lay there sobbing, in shock at what had just happened.

Very shortly afterwards Damien returned with a bunch of flowers. I had never had flowers bought for me before, they were beautiful. He was full of remorse telling me he was really sorry, and that he didn't mean it, he loved me so much he could not bear the thought of anyone else near me. I felt very flattered by what he said, almost touched really. I responded to his advances and reassured him that he had nothing to worry about. I explained again that we were only chatting to the builders. We

CHAPTER 9: DOUBTS

hugged and made up and things went along well for a little while, I was so in love with Damien and he with me.

Shortly after that first slap, Damien and I went to see his solicitor friend. I was told that he would get Stephanie back for me and that I was entitled to half of Jim's assets. I had never thought about that, I wasn't interested in his assets, I just wanted my baby back. Because Damien's solicitor was a private lawyer, I would have to pay a huge amount of money for him to represent me, money I didn't have. We decided to get a lawyer locally. The solicitor we got was very nice and very good, he told me he would do everything he could to get Stephanie back for me. I was delighted and I felt such relief.

I tried on several occasions to call Jim to speak with Stephanie, but he refused to let me, he would only give me a load of verbal abuse down the phone, but I kept trying in the hope that one day he would let me hear her voice. Then when I least expected it, he finally agreed to let me talk to her. I heard the wonderful sound of baby babble, I thought my heart would burst with the delight and the heartbreak I was feeling. I begged Jim to let me see her, even just for a short time, and to my surprise he agreed, laying down a load of conditions which I willingly agreed to, as all I wanted was to see my baby.

Within two weeks Damien and I arrived back in Ireland. I was so excited at the thought of seeing Stephanie. As I drove up the driveway of the house, I had knots in my stomach that you wouldn't believe. It had been nine long months since I saw my baby. I got out of the car and I thought my legs would buckle from under me, I knocked on the door and after what seemed like ages, the door opened, and standing there was my beautiful baby, no longer a baby but a gorgeous little girl.

As I gazed at this beautiful child she piped up in her broad accent 'you're my mammy.' I thought I would die on the spot, it was the first time I had heard her speak. Jim was very cold with me but I chose to ignore it, I was just so happy to see Stephanie. I had bought her a few dresses and I asked Jim if I put one on her. Going back into the house was really strange as I didn't feel anything for it any more. I got Stephanie dressed as she chatted happily to me looking deep into my eyes as she did so. I felt my heart was being squeezed, I was so happy, proud and heartbroken all at the same time.

We went to the beach for the day, Jim insisted on coming with me, as he didn't trust me not to snatch Stephanie. I have to be honest, that thought had crossed my mind many times. When I was in London I would lie awake for hours planning how I could get my baby back. But I was so frightened of getting into trouble I dared not do such a thing.

We headed off to the beach and although it was awkward with Jim, I chose to not let it spoil the wonderful time I was having with Stephanie. She was such a delightful child full of chat, full of life, I was enjoying every single second, and eventually even Jim relaxed a little more. When we got back to the house, I asked Jim if I could see Stephanie the next day. I was delighted when he agreed, and I felt that finally Jim and I could have some sort of civil relationship.

I returned to Damien and was full of non-stop chat about the wonderful time I'd had with Stephanie. I was exhausted but happily went to sleep so excited about the next day. As I drove up to the house again to see Stephanie I didn't feel nervous at all. I knocked on the door and waited for what seemed like ages, and when it finally opened I was met by a cold stony-faced

CHAPTER 9: DOUBTS

Jim. I smiled at him and asked where Stephanie was, and he very firmly and coldly told me she was where I couldn't see her. He said he had decided that I wasn't going to see Stephanie, if I wanted to see her I had to go thought the courts. He slammed the door shut in my face. I thought I was going to stop breathing.

I stood for a moment not believing what was happening. I knocked on the door again and begged Jim to please open the door, please talk to me, please let me see my baby. But there was no answer, then my little girl appeared at the window. I caught a brief glimpse of her as she waved to me before Jim pulled her away. I begged and begged Jim to let me see her just for a moment, but there was no answer. I sat on the doorstep and sobbed, I don't know how long I sat there but I finally conceded defeat and feeling totally broken I climbed back into my car. I don't remember the journey back to Damien, I was completely numb, I felt dead inside.

The next day we headed back to London and it was a very sombre and heartbreaking journey home. I fought back tears as flashes of Stephanie's little face and the sound of her sweet voice swam around in my head. I decided there and then I was going to give the fight of my life to get her back. I went to see my solicitor and told him what had happened, I told him I wanted to do everything that was possible to get Stephanie back. I also decided making sandwiches was not the job for me, so I went for an interview as a receptionist for a large company in north-west London, I was delighted when I was told I had got the job.

One day things were getting too much for me – I felt so lonely, I was missing Stephanie so much, and Damien was crushing me with his possessive behaviour. I decided to call my mother, and when I heard her voice I started to cry. I wanted to tell her about my heartbreak, I wanted to tell her how mean Damien was to me, but I didn't get a chance, she gave me a barrage of abuse for not telling her I was in London. She continued to tell me how bad things were for her in Ireland. She told me that some neighbours had heard about the abuse case and were targeting their house, making them live in fear. She said they were going to come to London and she asked me to sort things out for her. I became tongue-tied and couldn't speak properly, so I agreed to help them. Part of me was terrified at the thought of them coming over, and another part of me was pleased. I felt that as an adult they couldn't hurt me any more, I truly believed that we as a family could somehow heal the terrible fractures and pain that had happened, and I felt as an adult I could repair it all. How stupid can one person be?

When they arrived I had a flat arranged for them, not too far from where I lived. I felt really strange when I saw my stepfather – a feeling of pure hatred, but also a feeling of fear and childlike sadness for what he did to me – but I tried to put it all behind me and I thought I was doing a good job. I so wanted to be like a proper family, I so wanted to pretend that none of the abuse had happened. My mother was to plague me with demands and woes, and whatever she wanted I got for her, whatever she needed I sorted it out for her, all in the hope that I would gain her approval, all in the hope that she would love me. I didn't have much contact with my stepfather – he was always working and I would ensure that I didn't visit my mother when he was there. But on the occasions when I did see him I would make very sure that I was never alone with him.

CHAPTER 9: DOUBTS

I would sometimes feel sick at the way my mother constantly claimed her undying love for my stepfather, a voice would sometimes scream in my head, how could she love an abuser, how could she bear to be near him after what he did to his daughters and to me. It was not too long before I got to ask her those very questions in a situation that was to change my relationship with them for good. The situation was to traumatise me for many years as I finally realised just how evil they both were.

Back at home, because I didn't have a car of my own Damien would pick me up and drop me off at work. I noticed that he would always wait until I sat down at my desk before driving off, and he would arrive sometimes half an hour early to collect me, sitting right outside the window where he could see me clearly. The company I worked for was male dominated, so being the receptionist, sometimes the men would come to me and ask me to get a number for them, or they would stop by for general chit-chat. If Damien saw any man talking to me he would later give me the third degree as to what was said. I would have to go over it several times sometimes tripping over my words with the tiredness of repeating myself. If I did that Damien would get really mad, twisting and turning what I said until I didn't know what I was saying any more.

The pattern of this interrogation was to continue on an almost daily basis. He then would send me a bouquet of flowers almost every day to say he loved me. I thought that it was a lovely thing to do and convinced myself that he really did love me, but colleagues at work didn't see it quite the same way and would comment on Damien's behaviour. I would laugh it off saying that we were very much in love and this was just his way of showing it. Damien's controlling grip was getting ever tighter and I felt more and more helpless.

I couldn't understand why Damien would have sudden temper fits, he would be so aggressive and so uptight, his eyes like glass. Damien didn't have any work, he told me he used to work as a chauffeur many years before, so we decided that with the £10,000 I received from Jim, we would buy a car so he could do weddings. I would take the bookings and help him get the car ready for weddings every Saturday, and things were going well.

The pain of not having Stephanie was never far away. Papers were flying back and forth between Jim's solicitor and mine and it became very stressful. I remember being in a shopping centre one day and seeing a little girl that looked just like Stephanie, my heart jumped and then I realised it wasn't her. I dropped my bags of shopping and ran, I ran and ran sobbing for my baby, everywhere I seemed to look I saw little girls who looked just like my little girl, it was so hard to deal with. My divorce finally came through from Jim, but the custody case for Stephanie was to last for some years.

Chapter 10

A Second Marriage

In the spring of 1989, I found out I was pregnant again. I was over the moon, but when I told Damien he was less than pleased saying 'well that's that then isn't it?' It wasn't until I went for my first scan that he showed any interest in my pregnancy, he became very excited especially when we found out we were expecting a son. We got married that summer in a registry office in London, it was a very informal wedding but we had a good day, so I thought. Damien was knocking back Dom Perignon champagne like there was no tomorrow, and he kept disappearing to the bathroom with the best man. I didn't suspect a thing, even when they would return to the table and speak about Charlie I still had no idea what was going on. Other people at the table found it amusing and I could not work out what they were giggling about. It wasn't until we got back from our four-day honeymoon in Devon that I understood what was going on.

We had just bought our first flat together and we were very happy, my belly was getting bigger almost by the day and we were preparing for the birth of our son. I had stopped working because Damien told me to. But even then, I did not question anything, I never questioned where the money was coming from, I never questioned all the times he went out, whatever he told me I accepted. I was lost in my world of getting Stephanie back and preparing for our new baby.

One evening we had some friends of Damien's round for dinner. Everyone was drinking except me, and when we finished dinner, one of the guests asked Damien for desert. I stupidly said, 'sorry I didn't think to make one.' The guests all laughed at me and still I didn't get it. The next thing, Damien took out a small packet from his pocket, he got a mirror and a blade and his friend took out a £50 note and rolled it up like a straw. As Damien lined up this white powder on the mirror with such expertise, I felt very frightened, I still wasn't sure what was going on. I sat glued to my chair with fear as I watched one-by-one all our guests put this white powder up their noses. I was terrified and trying really hard not to cry. One of the guests turned to Damien and said that it was great Charlie. Now I got it, now I knew who and what Charlie was – cocaine. I felt sick. For all the trauma I experienced as a child, drugs had remained a huge no-no.

I sat very quietly as I watched Damien and our guests continue to put cocaine up their noses – the more they did, the louder they got, the more they talked. I looked at Damien with pleading, confused eyes, silently begging him to stop, but he just laughed.

When they had finished the cocaine, one of the guests rolled a cigarette, he took out a small piece of brown stuff from a piece of tin foil, to me it looked for all the world like turf from the bog. As he chatted he crumbled some of the brown stuff into his rolled up cigarette, he then sealed it up and lit it. I had never seen a cigarette like that before, nor had I ever smelt one like

CHAPTER 10: A SECOND MARRIAGE

that before. I sat and watched this cigarette being passed around the table. Curiosity got the better of me so I asked what cigarette it was – everyone laughed, I was mortified, and one of the female guests piped up 'sweety, it's a joint not a cigarette.' My face must have shown that I still didn't understand, so the woman said 'marijuana darling, you know?' I just smiled, inside I was hyperventilating with panic. Oh my God, these people take drugs and Damien takes drugs!

I didn't know what to do, I couldn't believe it, I had always associated drug-taking with the places I had lived in Dublin, yet here sat in front of me were highly-educated, highly-paid people. I thought they would never go home, I thought I would swallow my tongue with the things I wanted to say to Damien, the questions I wanted to ask. When everyone had left I turned to Damien and asked him what he thought he was doing bring drugs into our home? He just laughed at me and told me I was so stupid. I told him I did not want drugs in the house again, but he didn't like that, he got very mad, poking my shoulder and glaring at me he told me he would do what he liked when he liked. I was so frightened that he would hurt my unborn baby.

I went to bed in tears, I lay there and held my bump giving my unborn son a hug, scared of what was going to happen, and feeling so stupid that I had not noticed or questioned anything. As I lay there flashes of things that had happened popped into my head, all the times he went out, all the secret phone calls, all the times he would get angry – it was all starting to make sense, but how could I be that stupid that I didn't notice before? I decided I would talk to Damien and try and convince him to stop, we had everything to work for, a new home and a new baby on the way.

I tried several times to talk to him, but each time he got angry, so I stopped talking about it, hoping that he would see how much I loved him and that he would stop. I would try so hard to please him, when he went out in the evenings to do extra chauffeuring work, I would rush around cleaning our flat from top to bottom, I would cook a nice meal and have the table set with candles and a bottle of wine and some beers for him in the fridge. I would put on a pretty dress and make sure I looked as good as I could for him. I would then stand at the window with butterflies in my stomach waiting to see his car pull in and when he did I would be so excited – as he came through the door I would throw my arms around him and hug him for all I was worth. For a few months we were very happy, our happiness was complete when in November 1989 I gave birth to a beautiful bouncing baby boy. The first and only time I saw Damien cry was when he held our son Josh in his arms.

Josh was a complete delight, I loved him with every fibre of my being, all I wanted was to have Stephanie with me and I would be complete. When my son was about six months old Damien started to become more withdrawn from me – preferring to spend most of his time in the pub, he would start an argument, then storm out of the house leaving me with no money. He would take the keys with him so if I wanted to go out I wouldn't be able to get back into the house.

My son and I spent lovely times together when Damien was out, no shouting, no criticising, just laughter and peace. When Damien returned home he would be extremely drunk, he would barely be able to stand or speak clearly. He would start to pick on me to make me cry and then take a photograph of me crying.

CHAPTER 10: A SECOND MARRIAGE

I had got to the stage where I thought I couldn't live without him, where I really believed my entire survival depended on him. No matter how much he shouted at me, pushed me around, accused me, blamed me, all of which was totally unnecessary, I would end up saying sorry and begging him to forgive me for whatever it was I was supposed to have done. Our relationship was like a yo-yo – up and down all the time, it never stabilised for very long before the next outburst.

One evening in particular not long after Josh started walking, again there was an outburst, but somehow this was more frightening than usual, this evening he was furious. I was just getting Josh ready for bed when he came in from the pub very drunk, he was very agitated and started to pick on me, usually it would be because I didn't empty the bin, or our son's toys were still on the floor. It would always be over something and nothing, and I in turn would try and justify and explain myself, as I did on this particular evening. I put Josh to bed and as I was coming out of the bedroom, Damien pounced on me from nowhere, he was screaming at me, calling me the most horrendous names. He started to slap me quite violently around the head, I tried to protect myself by putting my hands up, but he pulled my hands out of the way, then he grabbed my hair. He was pulling it really hard, I begged him to stop, I begged him to please let me go, I kept saying 'I am sorry please don't hurt me', but he wouldn't stop. I could feel my face was wet, blood was streaming from my nose, he pulled my face close to his, and glaring at me with fire in his eyes, still calling me names, he pushed my head hard against the hallway wall. I just remember catching sight of Josh standing in the doorway of his room crying, he had only a few days before learnt how to climb out of his cot. I don't remember anything else as I fell to the floor.

I came round to the sound of Josh crying, he was standing over me calling my name, he was very upset. I tried to get up from the floor, but every part of me was in pain. My hair was covered in blood from my nose, my right eye was hurting, my whole body ached. I managed to get up, my head felt like it had a sledgehammer through it, I managed to get into the bathroom and clean myself up enough so that I could pick up my son. I held him so tight as he tried to pull away to look at me. I will never forget what he said to me that night 'mama sore, mama sore' as he pointed at my face. Fighting back tears I got him a drink and settled him back into his cot. Once I knew he was okay I went into the living room, I collapsed onto the sofa and I sobbed. How did it get to this? What did I do so wrong? What was I going to do? I had nowhere to go and no one to go to, I didn't want anyone to know what was happening, the shame of it all, I couldn't tell anyone. I had a bath and washed my hair, I was barely able to move with the pain, I was shaking from head to toe.

I heard the front door go and my heart nearly stopped, it was Damien, he was home, what was going to happen? I stayed in the bathroom with the taps running hoping that he would just go straight to bed, but he didn't. I heard a gentle knock on the bathroom door and a voice say 'Cas, Cassie, I am sorry, please come out.' I sat in the bathroom for a few minutes my heart beating so fast. I glanced in the mirror – my face was a mess. I went into the front room where Damien was sitting, my head held down, afraid to make eye contact with him. He jumped up and stood in front of me, I nearly died with fright, he held

CHAPTER 10: A SECOND MARRIAGE

my sore arms and kept pleading for me to look at him and telling me over and over again that he was sorry.

He gently guided me to the sofa and sat me down. He, with what sounded like genuine remorse, told me again how sorry he was, he tried to explain to me that he was under pressure with money, the mortgage was high and he was struggling to make the payments, he said he had seen a man that day in the pub who remarked on what a nice woman I was and he felt jealous. I found it hard to look at him, but at the same time could not help feeling sorry for the sad state that was sat next to me. Damien promised me he would never hit me again, he said he was going to make an effort to be a good man and the best husband he could be to me. He kept saying over and over he could not believe what he had just done to me, he kept saying sorry.

I decided that he meant what he said and our marriage was worth another try, anyway I was too exhausted and worn down to believe that I could survive by myself. But above all that, I really did love him.

For the next few weeks everything was good. I had a job to keep my mother away, she rang several times wanting to come and bend my ear, each time I had to think of an excuse for her not to come. I did not want her to see my face, as I knew that she would have some smart comment to make like 'you must have done something to deserve that.' I knew that she would not have the slightest compassion for me. So I felt it best to keep her away, the less she knew about me and Damien the happier I was. For those few weeks there seemed to be calmness in our home. My face had healed up okay and we were getting on fine. Damien wasn't going to the pub much, but when he did he would only go for a few pints and come straight home, he would sweep me in his arms and tell me how much he loved me, I gleefully would prepare his dinner and fuss around him like a love-struck teenager.

But that happiness did not last long. I was out shopping with Josh one day when I got chatting to one of the male shopkeepers, we were just having friendly banter, nothing out of the ordinary, in fact he was commenting on how much my son had grown. Unknown to me Damien had followed me to the shops, I didn't know he was standing behind me, when I saw him I got flustered and started to clumsily explain the conversation I was having. I quickly paid for my shopping and Damien and I headed out of the shop. He grabbed my arm and asked me 'what was all that about?' I tried to explain that we were only chatting. My explanation seemed to satisfy Damien and we headed home. Once we got indoors Damien said he was going to the pub, it was only the afternoon but that was not unusual for him. He said he was only going for a few pints and I had no reason to think different.

I went about my usual routine, sorting out Josh and preparing dinner. As the time went on and Damien wasn't home I started to get a bit worried but I convinced myself that I was worrying for nothing. When he did finally come home he was very drunk, I felt a little uneasy with him but chatted away about whatever popped into my head. Damien was clearly not listening to me. He went to the fridge and got himself another beer, and as he came back into the room he said 'so are you going to tell me what you and the bloke were really talking about today?' I had to think for a second, I had completely forgotten about the shop. I told him that we were just chatting

CHAPTER 10: A SECOND MARRIAGE

about Josh, I tried to remember word for word the conversation we had to relay it to Damien. As I was explaining I could feel my face getting hot and my hands were getting sweaty, I was very aware of the atmosphere in the room and could feel the tension screaming at me.

Without warning Damien jumped up and started to shout at me, calling me a whore, a dirty little whore. I froze, he grabbed me by the hair and started to slap my face. One of my neighbours was in his garden and could see through the patio doors what was going on. As Damien was screaming and shouting at me he punched me in the face causing my top lip to split, blood was everywhere. I was terrified, I somehow managed to get out of his grip and out of the front door and I ran, I had no shoes or socks on but I didn't care I just ran. I didn't know what to do, I was so scared he was coming after me, as I was running the neighbour who was in his garden came out after me and called me. I was hysterical, I thought it was Damien, I was disorientated and started to cry loudly, my neighbour grabbed me and led me towards his flat that he shared with his girlfriend. I was covered in blood, I had a white Aran jumper on that was just covered in blood.

My neighbour took me into his flat and told me he had seen everything that happened and had called the police. I panicked, I didn't want the police, what if they didn't believe me? What if they thought as Damien always said, it was my fault? What would happen to my son? All these questions were running through my head as my neighbour cleaned up my face. We saw the flashing blue lights of the police car, my heart was racing. I was terrified, what was going to happen?

My neighbour ran out to see the police and explained to them what was going on. A policeman came to see me and a policeman went into our flat. I was so scared seeing the uniform, and hearing his radio really frightened me. But he was so kind and gentle with me, I just kept saying over and over again that I wanted to be with my son. The policeman told me he would take me to him in a little while, he just wanted to ask me a few questions. He looked at my face and asked me what happened to it, he said it looked nasty and asked if I wanted to go to the hospital, he said my lip might need a stitch or two. I said, no thank you, I would be fine. Through blinding tears I told him what happened, I watched him write everything I said in his notebook.

The policeman disappeared for a few minutes and I wasn't sure what was going on. He returned and said it was safe for me to go back into my flat. I asked about Damien. The policeman told me he had been arrested for assault. My heart dropped I was so frightened, I hadn't experienced this before, we had always sorted it out ourselves. The policeman took me back into our flat. I went straight to check on Josh – he was fast asleep oblivious to what had just happened. I sat on the sofa and sobbed, my face was a mess, my life was a mess, I was so scared, everything felt too much for me.

I asked the police officers what was going to happen to Damien. They told me he would be kept in a cell overnight and would have to appear in court the next day. They started to tell me about injunctions and what that would mean, but it was up to me to have the final say if I wanted to take one out or not. If I did take out an injunction it would mean that Damien could not come near me, it meant that my son and I would be safe. I wanted to be safe of course, but how would I manage? How would I live? Damien had got me totally believing that I couldn't survive

CHAPTER 10: A SECOND MARRIAGE

without him. I thought for a few moments longer and agreed to get the injunction. I did not want Damien to hurt me anymore.

When the police had left I went to bed and cried myself to sleep. The next morning I woke to an empty bed, I lay there for a moment my face swollen and hurting as the reality of the events of the night before hit me like a ton of bricks. I really wanted to pull the duvet over my head and hoped that it was a bad dream and that it would all go away. But it wasn't a bad dream, this was my life. I rang my mother and very tearfully told her what had happened. I so wanted her to send some loving message down the phone to me, I wanted her to do that so much. She was less than sympathetic, telling me that I probably deserved it, she told me I should not provoke Damien. As I listened to her voice, I could feel my heart being squeezed again. How stupid could I be to expect any compassion from her? I put the phone down and a feeling of complete abandonment, loneliness and guilt hit me – maybe she was right, maybe it was all my fault, maybe I was all those things that she and Damien said I was.

For the next few weeks I just got on with looking after my son. I had no money as Damien had control over the money and had stopped me having access to the account. The money I got from Jim was well gone. I was penniless and frightened. Damien breached his injunction several times – he was not allowed to come any closer than the end of our road, but he would come and knock on the door begging me to have him back, he would constantly ring me, he would tell me how sorry he was and how much he loved me, he would get inside my head and make me believe that I couldn't live without him. I felt worn down and fully believed that I was inadequate and unable to cope, so I allowed him to come home on the condition that he would never hit me again and that the drugs would go.

For a while everything was okay, it was okay as long as I did what I was told when I was told, which I willingly did to keep the peace.

We decided to start our own media company and we both worked hard to get the business off the ground. Damien would still take cocaine and drink heavily. He would pick arguments and make me cry, crushing any confidence I had, but he hadn't hit me, so for me, I felt that life wasn't that bad. That was all to change one day when the reality of what was going on hit me hard.

I was preparing Josh's tea one evening and I gave him a carton of drink. I opened it for him and gave him the straw, but to my horror he straightaway put the straw to his nose and started sniffing the table. I quickly took the straw away and burst into tears, he just looked at me confused. I knew there and then something had to be done, I knew I most certainly did not want this for my son, but what could I do?

I confronted Damien and told him in no uncertain terms that his cocaine habit had to stop. I told him what Josh had done and that there was no way I was going to tolerate it any more. He promised me he would not bring cocaine into the house anymore and said he was very sorry, he was really going to make an effort. He did stop bringing cocaine home, but I knew he was still taking it. But I had become too exhausted and beaten down by him, the problems from my mother, the heartache I still felt for Stephanie, and Jim's total lack of co-operation to upset myself any further with Damien's misdemeanours.

Chapter 11

The Fight for Stephanie, and a New Baby

Finally a date came through to go to court regarding the custody of my daughter Stephanie. I was excited, but also dying inside with nerves. My solicitor had told me that it could go either way, that is how close it was. It had taken a few years to prove that the piece of paper Jim had tricked me into signing, was not worth the paper it was written on because I hadn't had any independent legal representation at the time.

But it was decided in court that because Stephanie was happy and settled at school in Ireland, it would be unfair to uproot her and move her to the UK. Instead it was agreed that I could have reasonable access to her six times a year. I was devastated that Stephanie would not be coming to live with me, the thought of having her just a few times a year was excruciating. As I stood in the courthouse looking at the delight on Jim's face, and the self-satisfied look of my solicitor I felt sick. I knew in my heart that Jim would not comply fairly with the court's decision. For once, I was right.

For the first year after the court agreement, things went along okay, in that Jim let me have Stephanie, when I was allowed to.

I would get so excited for each visit: preparing for her arrival; buying her clothes; boring my friends with all the things I would do with her when she arrived. I had to pay for all the flights and travel expenses which put a huge financial strain on Damien and I, and because I didn't have any financial independence I was totally depending on Damien to fund Stephanie's visits. He always did, but he would use it as a weapon against me. If he wasn't happy with something he would tell me I could f... off, he wasn't going to pay for my daughter to come over, why should he? She wasn't his. He would always keep me hanging until the last minute before he would allow me to book Stephanie's flights.

The stress of wondering each time if Damien was going to give me the money was horrible. I tried very hard not to let it get to me. I prayed and believed that Damien wouldn't let me down, he knew how much Stephanie's visits meant to me. I would fly into Dublin airport, and while the plane was being prepared for the return journey, I would run through the airport, my heart pounding, hoping against hope that Jim had showed up. Then I would get a glimpse of my little girl, my heart would lighten and a pool of love for her would just gush out of me. All the stress Jim caused me, all the stress Damien caused me, seemed to vanish into insignificance once I saw Stephanie. We would have lovely times together – my life and heart was complete when I saw Stephanie and Josh play together, when I was with them both I felt I hadn't a care in the world.

However, one day about a year later I got a call from Jim telling me that he had decided that Stephanie wasn't going to come to me anymore – he said that she was getting confused

CHAPTER 11: THE FIGHT FOR STEPHANIE AND A NEW BABY

and it wasn't in her best interests to come to London. I felt I had been stabbed in the heart. I begged him not to do it, I told him Stephanie needed both of us, but he wouldn't listen, he slammed the phone down. I tried to call many, many times, but each time I did, he would hang up the phone straight away. I had to go back to the solicitors and got into a further long and painful battle to see my daughter. Sometimes the pain was too much to bear.

My Little Star

Little darling, my bright star
I am here, I'm not far.
Close your eyes, and see my smile
I am sending you love, all the while.
The sea is between us, but it's just a pond,
No one can break our special bond.
So sleep well my darling, and know in your heart
I am beside you, although we're apart.

In October 1994, I was delighted to discover I was going to have another baby. Damien was less than pleased and chose not to get involved at all with my pregnancy, but I didn't care at the time because things were not great between us. I had found out that Damien was seeing other women, I'd found a pair of knickers on the bedroom floor that were definitely not mine, and when I confronted him he just laughed at me, telling me that it was no big deal, to relax it was just for sex. He told me that if I was any good he wouldn't have to do it. I was very upset and hurt. Again I felt totally inadequate and really believed I was no good.

I had a very stressful pregnancy this time. It was like Damien really hated me, I could do nothing right and everything wrong. He would spend the whole day in his office, then he would come home, grunt at me or start an argument before storming out, leaving me asking what it was that I did so wrong. He would sometimes come home late at night, and sometimes he would come home early the next morning. I just immersed myself in Josh and the pending birth.

When I went into labour this time, Damien decided that he didn't want to attend, he dropped me at the hospital door and drove off. I stood there for a moment looking after him as he sped out of the carpark, I felt so alone. When I reached the labour ward the nurse asked me where my partner was, and I very convincingly told her that he had been called away on business. A few hours later I gave birth alone to a beautiful baby boy, who I called Aaron.

I had not been home from hospital long, when the violence started again. Aaron was a little difficult and would cry a lot. This really annoyed Damien – he would stomp around, then he would storm out of the house and be gone for hours. I didn't mind, in actual fact I was quite pleased to get some peace and quiet.

Aaron was about one month old when a friend asked if I would like to go out for a drink. I hadn't been out for what seemed like ages, so I asked Damien if I could go, and he agreed to mind the boys. I put on my gladrags and make-up and my friend and I headed to the local pub. It felt so great to be out, I

CHAPTER 11: THE FIGHT FOR STEPHANIE AND A NEW BABY

loved the buzz of all the people around me, everyone seemed so happy and confident, everything I wasn't. My friend and I had a great time chatting and having a few drinks, and we were quite giddy as we made our way home. We decided to go through the park and laughed and chatted the whole way. When I got home I was feeling happy, I'd had a wonderful time. I didn't notice that my shoes had mud on them from the park. I thought Damien would have been in bed but he was waiting for me in the living room. I could sense an atmosphere straight away, so I tried to humour him with tales of my evening out.

Damien was listening intently as I waffled on, but he suddenly stopped me mid-sentence and asked me what mud was doing on my shoes. I light-heartedly told him about the walk home through the park, but Damien told me he did not believe me. He started to shout at me. 'Who were you with? Who is he?' He accused me of being with a man in the park and no matter how much I protested he kept shouting.

I was very upset that he would think such a thing, and I was very frightened as he came right up to my face and continued shouting. He grabbed my arms and started to shake me, calling me names. I was terrified, I was sobbing and begging him to please leave me alone I really didn't do anything wrong, but he wouldn't listen.

He slapped me hard across the face, then he dragged me into the bedroom and raped me, telling me I could give him what I'd given the bloke in the park. I lay there frozen inside, my body limp like a rag doll, I didn't make a sound. With tears steaming down my face I reacted exactly as I had done as a child.

The next day, I felt totally broken. I didn't believe my heart could be broken anymore than it was at that very moment. How could the man I loved, the father of my children do such a horrid thing to me? How could he want to hurt me like that? I looked at my two boys, Aaron babbling away at Josh. I couldn't control my tears. I felt trapped and desperate.

I thought, 'I have to do something.' I went to the police and told them what had happened, and again an injunction was taken out. This time Damien decided to contest it which put the fear of God into me. I had to go to court which was very scary. Damien had decided to represent himself, and when the allegations were put to him, he stood across from me and as he spoke he never took his eyes off me. I was choking back the tears as I heard him utter the words 'any injuries my wife received sexually were inflicted on her by the man she had sex with in the park.' He totally denied that he had done anything to me.

The judge didn't believe him – he said there was not enough evidence for a rape charge, but because of Damien's history he would serve the injunction. I got some relief from knowing that he couldn't come near me, but I was highly ashamed and hurt at his nasty denial. As I was walking back to my car I heard my name being called, and I turned to see Damien smiling at me. I told him to leave me alone, quickly jumped in my car and drove off shaking from head to toe.

Just like last time, Damien stopped everything at the bank so the boys and I had no money. I thought I would be strong and once and for all stand on my own two feet, so I went to the welfare office and was able to sort out some money. Although it was not a lot it was better than nothing, and the boys and I were safe and happy, as far as I was concerned I felt like I had won the lottery.

CHAPTER 11: THE FIGHT FOR STEPHANIE AND A NEW BABY

Damien and I had been apart for a couple of months and I really believed that he had gone for good. I was slowly piecing the fragments of my life back together again. It was Bonfire Night and the boys and I were invited to a firework display with some friends. We had a lovely time – although I had little money I felt as free as a bird. My mother was also giving me some space because I had no money and two children, so I was of no real use to her, for me that was a blessing in disguise.

When the boys and I arrived home that night I noticed as soon as I walked in, the flat was extremely cold. I knew I had left the heating on because Aaron was only three months old and I was worried that he would catch a cold. I went around the flat wondering if I had left a window open, I nearly died when I went in to my bedroom and saw the curtain flapping in the wind. The window had been smashed and all my mail had been taken. I was so frightened, I immediately called the police, not for one second thinking it was anything other than a random break-in.

When the police arrived they asked me if anything else had been stolen, but it was only my mail. They then asked me if there was anyone I knew who might do such a thing, as it was very unusual for a burglar to just steal someone's mail. My heart sank, the only person who would do that was Damien, but why? I told the policeman about Damien and he felt sure it was likely to have been him, but it could be hard to prove. He suggested that I get someone to fix the window, and told me not to leave my mail in view anymore.

My peace of mind was shattered from that moment on. I couldn't sleep. I had to sell my car to pay the bills and when I was walking Josh to school I was sure I was being followed. I wasn't wrong. Damien would call me, and would tell me what I was wearing, who I had been speaking to, the time I got home, he knew everything about me. I was terrified. Then he changed tack and would tell me how much he missed me and the boys, begging me to have him back, promising he would change, telling me that he loved me, telling me it was not right for the boys to grow up without their father, it was not fair that they had no money. If I had him back he would make sure we were alright for everything, he would take good care of us. I wrestled and wrestled with what to do, a huge part of me still loved him and I desperately wanted family life. I did not want to be a single parent, so I had him back.

Chapter 12

Confrontations

Everything went along okay for a while. We moved to a bigger house, the business was doing well, and the boys seemed happy, although Aaron was a real handful. I busied myself making our house into a home and being a good wife and mother, and I was also working in the business. Damien seemed a bit more settled and less aggressive. My mother now had further to travel to see me, so I saw less of her which was only a good thing for me. Then one day I was to get the shock that would change things between my mother and I forever.

My mother arrived at the house with my younger sister Sheila and my stepfather. My mother was in tears and my stepfather had a stony look about him. I knew something was wrong, but I wasn't prepared for what was to come. My mother proceeded to tell me that Patricia had called at the flat and confronted her father about the abuse. She said that Patricia would not let it go until he admitted what he had done. I could feel my throat closing, my knees going weak and I thought I would collapse. But somewhere inside me I was thinking 'Why am I feeling like this? Surely this is a good thing. Once and for all we don't have to carry this terrible lie anymore?' As I listened to my mother, I could feel my stepfather's gaze on me. My mother continued, saying Patricia just wouldn't leave until she got an answer.

I was frightened and uncomfortable, but something swelled deep inside me at that moment. I turned to my stepfather and looked him straight in the eye and asked, 'and what did you say?' He hung his head and started to cry and said, 'I admitted it, I admitted I abused you all, but you the most.' I didn't know what to say – I was frozen to the spot, and the anger and hatred I felt for him at that moment was overwhelming. I saw crying before me a pathetic excuse for a man, and I thought 'good, you cry, you cry like I cried when you stole my innocence and childhood away from me, you cry, but I know you will never cry like I have done.' As I looked at him I knew that he was crying for himself, crying that he'd been found out at last.

My mother looked at me and said, 'Look at the state of your poor father. Tell me it's not true Cas, tell me it's all lies.' I turned to my mother and said, 'No mam, it's not lies, it's all true. He raped me from when I was very young until I was sixteen.' Looking straight at my stepfather I said, 'Didn't you?' and still crying he nodded. My mother became hysterical and ran out into the garden. I went out after her to try and calm her down, but she grabbed me as she had done when I was a little girl, she glared at me and said, 'I can't believe you slept with my husband.' She gave me a hard slap across the face and continued, 'you're a dirty, dirty whore, you hear me? A dirty little whore! I never want to see you again, you disgust me!'

I was in complete shock. I couldn't believe how she had reacted. I felt my heart was being squashed again, and standing there like a child I said, 'But mammy, I was just a little girl, your little girl and he did all those things to me.' She came right up

CHAPTER 12: CONFRONTATIONS

to my face and said 'You're no child to me, as far as I am concerned you are dead to me.'

I stood there sobbing as she, my stepfather and Sheila stormed out. I rubbed my face and sat on the ground thinking, 'How could my mother say that? How could she reject me like that? How could she hate me so much? What did I do to make her hate me?' I was devastated – the feeling of abandonment was crushing. Even though I knew she didn't really like me, it was not until I looked in her eyes that day that I realised just how much she actually hated me. It took many years for me to come to terms with that day and that final rejection.

When Damien came home that night he could see I was very upset and I told him what had happened. He didn't say too much other than 'that's terrible'. But he would throw that day in my face many times after that, saying 'your own mother didn't even want you, she was right, you are a dirty little whore.' That was like having a knife stuck deep inside me and turned several times. No matter how often he said it, it hurt the same every time.

In December 1997, I found out I was pregnant again. This time I was having a little girl and I was over the moon – it somehow felt I had been given a second chance. The visits from Stephanie were few and far between, despite her being older now and allowed to decide for herself, which was still very difficult for me. Anytime I would see her she seemed to be growing up so fast and was sometimes rather distant towards me. I had missed out on so much of her growing up.

So Lizzy was born in August 1998 and she was a gorgeous blue-eyed beauty. Damien was there at her birth, but against his will. While I was in labour he asked me how long I would be because he had to get straight back to the office to send a fax. I told him I was going as fast as I could, but it wasn't up to me, it was up to our baby and she would come when she was ready. Within half an hour of her birth Damien left, I didn't mind too much though, I was just besotted with my new daughter.

That night when she was asleep, I went into the hospital gardens, looked up at the stars and thanked God for giving me another chance to raise a little girl. I promised God that I would love her and look after her forever.

When I got home from hospital, I found coping with three children difficult. Aaron was very demanding and exhausting, and Josh was doing various after-school activities which I would take him to. Damien wasn't hands-on at all with the children, and I was very much like a single parent. I would get very tired, sometimes exhausted, trying to run the house and work in the business. I couldn't understand why I was crying all the time, and this really annoyed Damien. He had no patience with me, and I had to try to hide it from him, and with practice I did. When Lizzy was three months old I was diagnosed with post-natal depression.

Looking back I am not so sure it was all post-natal depression – to say I was depressed would be correct, but it was as much situational as anything else. I was still very traumatised from my mother's last visit. I was still being abused by Damien – the police had been to our house so many times by this stage, and I would tell them to take him away for the night, but I would always have him back the next day. I was broken physically and emotionally. I truly believed that I could not live without him. I did not have the energy to fight him – he was such a scary man, I knew I could never win against him. I also really wanted

CHAPTER 12: CONFRONTATIONS

to have a complete family: Mum, Dad and the children, and that was the most important thing to me, even at the cost of my own happiness, I truly believed I could make it work. I convinced myself I was strong enough to handle it all and that Damien didn't mean to hurt me – anyway, like he said, it was probably all my fault, I brought it all on myself.

After Lizzy was born I decided to get sterilised, as I thought at that time I did not want anther child. Damien had so much power over me when I was pregnant, and he loved the idea of my time being caught up with the children, as it gave him more time to do what he wanted.

In December 1998 my world was again turned upside down. One day I got up early with the children preparing for Christmas. I had asked Josh to empty the bin for me, but it was too full and heavy so we emptied some of the rubbish into another bag. I came across some small pieces of paper, neatly torn and piled on top of each other. I looked at them, and put them on the breakfast bar and jigsawed them together. My heart started beating faster as I realised it was a hotel bill with Damien's signature on it from only a couple of days before.

I had that sick feeling again, as I looked at the Christmas tree and all the lights and looked at our three children playing. I didn't know what to do. But something inside said I had to know, I had to deal with this and maybe my fears were totally unfounded. I went into the bedroom where Damien was watching TV and I put the small bits of paper in front of him on the bed. I asked him to explain them to me because my head was running away with me. He started to laugh, and told me to stop making a big deal out of things, it was nothing. He grabbed the papers and scrunched them up, but I wouldn't let it go. He came out with a million excuses, each one I knew was a lie. He eventually told me that he had gone to the hotel to have sex with a prostitute, and asked me if I was satisfied now that I knew.

No, I was not satisfied at all, in fact I was devastated, how could he do that to me and to our children? What did I do that he felt the need to do that? He would not answer any of my questions. I had to put on a brave face for the children, so I just got on and did what I had to do, but tears were never far from my eyes. We had been invited out for dinner that evening and I wanted to cancel, I didn't think I could face a room full of people. But Damien convinced me to go. I couldn't look at Damien, every time I heard his voice or his laugh it made me cringe. How could he laugh knowing what he had done? But deep inside I knew he didn't care about my feelings, all he cared about was being found out. When we got home and the children were in bed, Damien tried to talk to me. I didn't want to look at him, I didn't want to listen to him telling me it was my fault he had to use a prostitute, because I was so inadequate. Why did he hurt me so much?

Christmas came and the children did help me to enjoy it, seeing the beaming smiles on their little faces as they opened their presents, and the gleeful squeals as they got more excited with every parcel they opened. As for Damien and I, well, we didn't communicate much. Damien kept making advances, but I just couldn't bear him to touch me, I would freeze when he came near me. He would clumsily try to tell me he was sorry, but always end the conversation blaming me.

I tried very hard not to listen, but it gnawed away at me that just maybe it was my fault. Maybe I was all the things he said I

CHAPTER 12: CONFRONTATIONS

was, maybe I was all the things my mother and stepfather said I was. The torture of feeling my very existence was the reason for all that was wrong was so crippling. I could feel myself becoming more insular, I could feel any confidence I had slowly slipping away. I would take the children to the park, or to the supermarket, and I would look around at all the people there and an overwhelming feeling of inadequacy would grip me. How come everyone else seemed so happy? How come everyone seemed to be getting it right and I was getting it so wrong?

The fighting still continued. If I asked for housekeeping money I might as well have asked for a million pounds. If I went out I would be questioned over and over again, constantly being accused of being with other men. Damien's obsession with me became terrifying. I would get defensive and shout at him to leave me alone and of course the children would hear me shouting – Damien had a knack of being very angry and horrible without raising his voice, so the children only ever heard me.

One day a friend of Damien's came to me and confessed that he had been paid to follow me. I knew that Damien followed me regularly, but now he was paying other people to do it. I felt so scared, I soon didn't go anywhere other than to do normal things like shopping or school runs. It was exhausting looking over my shoulder all the time.

One of the most controlling things Damien ever did was to bug our house. I had some friends around for a drink and we were just chatting about everything and anything as a group of women do. When my friends had left, I put the children to bed. Shortly after Damien came back with a small audio tape in his hand, and started to shout that my friends and I were dirty whores. He had heard everything, and said I was nothing more than a gutter whore. He jeered at me, telling me I was a state, no one would want me, no one could love me, I was nothing. I was making a fool out of him, he only stayed with me because he felt sorry for me. As these words rang out, I felt crushed, totally degraded and useless – was he right? Was I really all those things?

Damien stormed out. I was very shaken, I sat for a while looking at our lovely home, the home I had lovingly created, I looked at the photos of my smiling children and I just sobbed. I was desperately unhappy, I felt trapped and alone and I was full of despair. All that kept me going was my children, and I thanked God every day for them.

When I finally went to bed, I fell into a deep exhausted sleep. I didn't hear Damien come home or enter the bedroom, but I was abruptly awakened by him shaking me hard, he was calling me a dirty whore over and over again. I was disorientated, I didn't know what was going on. Damien hissed at me that I was going to give him what I was giving all the other men I fucked. I begged him please not to do this, I pleaded with him, I tried to tell him that he'd got it all wrong, I hadn't been with other men, but he didn't listen. I lay there as I had done so many times before in my life, totally detached from my body, tears streaming down my face, but my ability to go into my dreamworld was gone. All I saw when Damien did that to me was a very dark hole and I was in the middle of it with no way to escape.

Chapter 13

An Unexpected Pregnancy

As the new millennium approached, I watched almost from the outside of life, people getting excited, preparing for this historic event. I couldn't get excited because for me I felt nothing was ever going to change – although I tried hard to believe that things would change, deep down I knew that they wouldn't. What I didn't know was that very early in 2000, I was going to get news that was to turn my world even more upside down than it already was.

I hadn't been feeling well for a few weeks and thought I had a tummy bug of some sort. I hadn't had my period for a while but thought nothing of it, as since I had been sterilised my periods had been all over the place anyway. I happened to mention this illness to a friend of mine on the phone on New Year's Eve and she asked me if I was sure I wasn't pregnant. I laughed and told her not to be silly, I had been sterilised, there was no way I could be pregnant. She told me that was not necessarily true, she had read somewhere about a woman who had got pregnant after being sterilised. As my friend was saying all this to me I felt I had been hit by a truck. No way, I couldn't be pregnant, I couldn't cope with another baby, not the way things were with Damien. I knew that I would be more trapped than I already was, so I totally dismissed the idea that I could be pregnant.

But in the early part of 2000, I did a test and my greatest fear was confirmed. There, staring back at me was a perfectly clear blue line. My heart sank. I went into a panic with a million hows running through my head. How could I be pregnant, I had just been sterilised four months before? What was I going to do? How would I cope? I sat and sobbed looking at this blue line. If I had a happy home and a loving supportive husband I would have never been sterilised, but I knew that bringing another baby into our lives was definitely not a good thing for me.

When I told Damien he was not happy. We went to the hospital and had a meeting with a senior consultant who scanned me to confirm I was pregnant, and as I looked at the tiny foetus sitting in my womb I knew there and then that I wanted that baby. Damien had tried a couple of times to get me to change my mind and have a termination, but there was no way after seeing my baby I was going to do that.

I had a very difficult pregnancy, I spent quite a lot of time in and out of hospital, but most of the difficulties were caused by the stress and tension in our house. Damien was becoming more possessive and paranoid, more critical and more controlling than ever. He would regularly make me cry and the threat of a slap was never far away. I was living on my nerves. I tried to shut myself off from him as much as I could.

I decided to research as much as I could about failed sterilisations and was shocked to find out the statistics. I set up a small support group for women like myself who found themselves pregnant after being sterilised. It was amazing how many women felt as I did, guilty, angry, frightened. Everything

CHAPTER 13: AN UNEXPECTED PREGNANCY

I was feeling I was hearing from other women over and over again. Damien hated the fact that I was doing something independent from him, he would give me such a hard time, telling me I was wasting my time and what I was doing was useless. I chose not to listen to him and continued with my support group.

I went into labour at seven months and I was told by the doctors that my baby was a little girl who had a very poor chance of survival because she was so small. At that moment I knew I was totally in love with this baby and I wanted her more than anything. The doctors gave me drugs to stop the contractions which thankfully worked. For the remainder of my pregnancy I was under the watchful eye of the hospital. In early August of 2000 I went into labour. It was late in the evening, and all the children were asleep. Damien had gone to bed, and I was pacing the kitchen waiting until I knew it was time to go to the hospital.

I went upstairs and called Damien, I told him it was time to go to the hospital. He sleepily turned to me and told me he was too tired to take me. I thought he was joking, but he wasn't. I picked up my hospital bag and with angry disbelieving tears, I put the baby seat in the car and drove myself to the hospital. The contractions were coming hard and fast as I pulled into the car park. I made my way to the labour ward and was greeted by a lovely nurse. She asked me if I had someone with me, and once again I said my husband had been called away unexpectedly on business. I told her I was fine and made light of the situation as much as I could, but I can say I never felt as lonely as I did that night.

Within an hour of getting to the hospital I was holding my beautiful new daughter, Hope. She was so tiny I thought I would break her, I was only allowed to hold her briefly. Because she was so small she had to be put in an incubator for a little while. As I looked at this tiny body lying there I truly believed that she was my miracle baby. She was so beautiful, a mop of black hair and big brown eyes. When the nurses brought her back to me and we were left alone in the room, I started to cry. I was so sad that I had no one to share this moment with – as I looked at my baby I felt a deep deep love for her, and a fear from knowing just how much she depended on me. I knew I had to be strong.

I asked the nurse for an early discharge after just six hours, as it was Lizzy's second birthday and I had arranged a party for her. I told the nurse that I needed to get home. She found it quite extraordinary that my two girls shared the same birthday, and I joked with her telling her it was very careful planning to cut down on birthday parties. I got the six hour discharge and before I was asked too many questions about who was collecting me, I quickly gathered up my paperwork and left, putting my baby carefully in the car and heading to the supermarket to get party food. I arrived home and the other children were so excited about their new sister, but when Damien came in from the office, he didn't ask me how I was or say very much at all. I took our new daughter out of her crib and introduced him to her. I offered her to him but he wouldn't hold her. I told him what I had called her, he told me it was a stupid name, turned on his heels and walked out.

People started to arrive for Lizzy's birthday party and were shocked to see I'd had the baby and was already home. I made light of everything and avoided any questions about Damien's involvement. That evening when everyone had left I was totally

CHAPTER 13: AN UNEXPECTED PREGNANCY

exhausted, I'd had no sleep for almost 24 hours. I started to bleed quite heavily and felt most unwell, but I kept going until I had all my chores done.

Within a few days of the birth, I noticed that Hope had a lot of involuntary muscle movement in her arms and legs, so I mentioned it to the midwife when she came to visit. She immediately said she wanted her to see the GP who would probably refer her to a specialist. She reassured me there was probably nothing to worry about, the shaking could possibly be due to her low birth weight. I tried not to worry, but it was very hard, Hope was shaking almost all of the time and she cried most of the day and night. I was getting no help from Damien at all – I would have loved him to take her just for an hour so I could get some much needed sleep, but no, he wouldn't do it. I was surviving on three to four hours sleep a night and Hope would not stop crying, no matter what I did for her it didn't seem to soothe her.

One night I was so exhausted I sat on the kitchen floor holding Hope in my arms as she cried and cried. I was crying too, I just didn't know what to do. Damien came storming into the kitchen and told me to shut the baby up as he was trying to sleep. I wanted to kill him at that moment, I didn't even look at him as I just sat there sobbing trying to comfort my baby.

Within a very short time I was to be dealt a terrible double blow. Hope was diagnosed with mild right hemiplegia and epilepsy. I was devastated as the doctor explained to me that what she had was a form of cerebral palsy. As he was explaining to me how it would affect her not only now but for the rest of her life, I couldn't take it all in. I went into shock. My baby was disabled, how could that be? What did I do wrong when I was pregnant? Could I have prevented this? Immediately the guilt set in and an overwhelming feeling of protection towards my daughter. I came home from the hospital heartbroken as I realised the enormity of care and help she would need. I wanted to wrap her up and hold her for as long as I could. I wanted to fix her, but I knew I couldn't.

A few days after that I was dealt the second bombshell. Aaron was, as I have already mentioned, a bit of a handful. He would have terrible temper tantrums and often behaved strangely. His nursery called me in one day and explained their concerns, and they asked if I would agree to have him assessed at the child development unit, to see if he may have a learning difficulty. I didn't think too much about it and agreed to do whatever was needed.

After his assessment I was called to a meeting at the child development unit to meet the various people who had assessed Aaron. As I listened, one by one each person explained to me the difficulties my son had. In conclusion, they all agreed that he was autistic, he had Asperger syndrome to be exact. I could feel my head swimming. How could I have missed all these things? How could I not have known that there was something wrong with my son? As things were being explained to me I couldn't take it in, I had never heard of autism before.

Appointments were made for Aaron to receive different therapies, hands were shook and I headed home with all the children. As I looked in the rear view mirror at the four little faces, I knew there and then my job was to be the best mother I could possibly be, I knew that my life was going to be committed to taking extra care of Aaron and Hope. Tears welled in my eyes as the enormity of the task ahead became a reality.

CHAPTER 13: AN UNEXPECTED PREGNANCY

That evening when the children were in bed, I sat with Damien and told him what the doctors had said about our son. I tried to explain it to him as it was explained to me, but at every step he would interrupt me and try to twist what I was saying. I started to get flustered and I burst into tears, I got very upset and said I didn't know how I was going to cope with two children who had special needs. I blurted out that I felt it was my fault they had problems, maybe I did something wrong when I was pregnant. I was so distraught, and not thinking about what I was saying. Damien became very impatient with me and jumped up, shouting that there was nothing wrong with the children, I was just an attention-seeking bitch who had brought all this on herself. He then stormed out, and I sat there in tears as I looked at my baby daughter who had for a short while stopped crying. I held her so tight and thanked God for giving her to me. I prayed so hard that God would give me the strength to deal with what lay ahead. I prayed to him to give Damien patience, to give him the skills to support me, to make him see what he was doing to me and to stop. But my prayers seemed to fall on deaf ears, for things were to get worse. I would come to regret sharing my feelings with Damien that night because he would use what I said against me at every opportunity after that.

I would beg Damien for help. I would spend two or three days at the child development centre with either Aaron or Hope. I was exhausted trying to keep up with all the therapies, and I would be given a list of activities to do at home with them as well. The days didn't seem to have enough hours in them to do all that I needed to do, plus Damien expected me to keep working in the office, but he would give me no help in the house.

Dealing with my son's behaviour and my daughter's epilepsy was very difficult, but my other two children were great. If Hope was having a fit Josh knew what to do, and he was also wonderful with his brother – he was so patient with him and would spend a long time helping him to accomplish small tasks. Lizzy was a wonderful child, and she never caused me a minute's trouble. I guess she had an inbuilt radar that told her I would get to her when I could. My younger son and daughter were so demanding, sometimes I only got to do the practical stuff with her, but she never complained or demanded.

Somehow the children and I managed to get through each day fairly intact, some days were better than others, but on the whole we were okay. Damien had distanced himself from the children, he didn't get involved at all. I felt a sense of guilt for Josh, he felt he had a responsibility towards his brother and me, and he would help me as much as he could, doing more than most young boys of his age. The children and I were very close. When Damien was out we could and would have fun. When Damien came back in, the whole atmosphere in the house would change.

Hope was about four months old and I was so tired. I'd had a day from hell: the baby never stopped screaming; Aaron had knocked Lizzy out of her highchair giving her a huge bump on her head; she was crying; Aaron started screaming because things were not going his way; Josh became upset saying 'why couldn't he have a normal family?'

I was in a bit of a heap when a nosy woman from the local pub knocked on the door saying she wanted to see the new baby. I stupidly invited her in, I could smell drink on her breath, but didn't say anything. Damien came in from work and they both

CHAPTER 13: AN UNEXPECTED PREGNANCY

chatted like old friends, flirting with each other in front of me, but I was too exhausted to care. I had just finished feeding Hope and was changing her nappy. I had no nappies in her baby bag, so I asked Damien to keep an eye on her while I fetched some from upstairs. She had a slightly sore bottom, but no worse than any of my other children had had and I was treating it with cream. But when Damien noticed her bottom he started to shout at me in front of this woman telling me how negligent I was, then the woman came to have a look and started to shout at me too. I couldn't believe it, the woman in no uncertain terms shouted at me to get up the fucking stairs and get the child a nappy.

I went upstairs desperately upset. How dare she speak to me like that? Why did everyone think they had a right to shout at me like I was stupid and incompetent? As I was coming down the stairs I could hear them saying horrid things about me. From nowhere I got this urge to run, so I opened the big window at the top of our stairs, threw the nappy over the banisters, climbed out of the window and I ran. I ran and I ran, sobbing, I felt I was losing my mind, I felt desperate. I ended up on a park bench in town, sobbing with no coat on. I knew I should be at home with my children, but I knew if I went back Damien and that horrible woman would continue with their barrage of abuse. I was frightened and angry, if I could have screamed for help I would have, but I was too heartbroken to open my mouth.

I spent that night in the park, afraid to go home and freezing, feeling like the loneliest person on the planet. As it was getting light I slowly walked home dreading what I would face, and I was right to feel like that. Damien was furious, the verbal abuse he gave me that morning was vile, he did not believe that I'd spent the night in the park, he was convinced I'd spent the night with a man. The abuse he gave me was unbelievable. I tried not to listen to him, but his voice had this way of getting into my head and making me believe everything he said was true.

A few days later, I had another exhausting day and I was feeling as broken as I could do. I was functioning like a robot, doing things that needed doing and then not remembering that I had done them and doing them again. I felt like I was going mad. Damien was probably right – I was all the things he said I was. Like he said, even my own mother didn't like me. Finding the hotel bill receipt had affected me more than I could explain – although I knew Damien was seeing other women, somehow having it thrust in my face like that hurt me more than I realised.

I had become very distant from Damien, his very presence made me close up physically and emotionally. I didn't have anything to say to him, just tears and anguish which sent us into a spiralling round of arguments, so much so that I thought we had reached the point of no return. I could see my family unravelling in front of my eyes. I truly believed that I would be better off without him and that the children and I would be a lot happier. Finally I spoke to Damien and told him that it was over once and for all, that I could no longer put up with what was happening. He begged and begged me not to split the family up, he told me once again that he would change and to prove it he would give me the wedding I never had in a church, we would renew our marriage vows and he would prove to me just how much he loved me.

Damien told me how sorry he was for hurting me, he promised that he would never do it again, no more drugs, no

CHAPTER 13: AN UNEXPECTED PREGNANCY

more women, no more beatings, no more lying. I really wanted to believe him. I really wanted to make our marriage work. I really wanted to keep my family together. So I gave him the benefit of the doubt, truly believing that we could make it.

Chapter 14

Slipping

So, in February 2001, we had our youngest daughter, Hope, christened, and renewed our vows at the same time. I felt so happy and proud to see all my friends and children there. When we got to the reception I was on such a high, the day was going so well, and I really felt that this was a new beginning. I looked around the room and felt happy and proud. Damien started to drink quite heavily, and I became a little uneasy, but dismissed my anxiety because the day seemed so perfect. I was busy chatting to people, but I noticed Damien kept disappearing. I tried not to let it bother me, but I soon had that sick feeling again, knowing deep inside what he was up to. I chose to ignore it and decided that this was a special day and I was not going to let anything spoil it.

As the evening wore on I noticed that Damien was a little worse for wear, and that sick feeling was never far away from me. I was right to feel anxious. I was talking to one of my friends and her boyfriend, we were chatting and laughing, when I felt this sudden terrible pain in my head. Damien had grabbed me by the hair and was dragging me, he threw me on to the floor and stamped hard on my face, he started to kick me in the back calling me the most horrendous names. Guests had to come and pull him off me. As I lay there bleeding and shaking, I felt my whole world collapse down around my ears. Any love I had for Damien slowly seeped out of me that day as I looked at the hatred for me he had in his eyes. People fussed over me with pure pity, I wanted to scream at them to leave me alone, I wanted to run again, I wanted to run away to die, my heart was in pieces.

In aftermath of that day, a huge part of me died inside. I felt so trapped, so desperate, so alone, where could I go with four children? My mother hated me, my relationship with my sisters was broken because of the abuse, I had no aunts, uncles, cousins, I had no one. I was stuck and Damien knew it and loved that fact.

Very shortly after that day, I did something drastic that was not just a cry for help, but a means of escape and an end to the desperation I felt. Things between Damien and I were as bad they could be. I no longer felt anything for him at all. I lost interest in almost everything that I loved – my writing, my music, my friends – nothing seemed important to me any more except the children.

I immersed myself in the therapies that would help Aaron and Hope. I refused to believe that either of them would have anything less than a normal quality of life with their disabilities. I refused to believe that they could not live full independent lives. I worked hard with them both and slowly the results started to show.

Although I was doing all these things, I could feel myself slipping into a very dark hole that had no way out. I tried to pull out of it, but instead I slipped further and further until I really felt that I was losing my mind. I felt like the worst person in the world, a complete failure, and all I seemed to do was let

My Wedding Day

A monster tried to kill me today, on this, my wedding day,
He grabbed my hair, threw me down on the floor,
He started to kick me, then kicked me some more,
'Please don't hurt me' I started to cry,
With his boot on my face, I thought I would die.

The pain I was feeling was more than before,
As he put his boot in to kick me some more,
People came running to pull him away,
On this, my wedding day.
Gone were the vows, the pretty dress,
My body, my face, my heart in a mess,
I came home quietly all broken and worn,
Worrying stupidly, was my dress torn.
I went upstairs, slipped out of my dress,
I looked in the mirror, my face was a mess.

I crept downstairs to fetch a drink.
'He'll be sleeping now' is what I did think.
I went to the kitchen, and out of the blue,
He grabbed me again 'I'm not finished with you'
He punched and he kicked me, threw me around,
I lay injured, curled on the ground.

CHAPTER 14: SLIPPING

> The memories of my wedding day, strong in my mind,
> That saying is true 'love is blind'
> So here am I with a band on my finger,
> As I sat there alone how those words did linger,
> For better, for worse, till death us do part
> This was supposed to be a new start.
> But once again I'm alone in tears,
> Still being battered, its been going on years.

Damien upset me. I was constantly defending myself and trying to justify my very existence. One evening I was sitting in the kitchen crying at the enormity of my situation, when a dark feeling of desperation came over me. I picked up a photo of all the children together and I looked at their beautiful faces. I felt I was such failure to them all, I felt I had let them down and they deserved better.

I had decided that they would be better off without me, so I took a pen and some paper and wrote a letter to each of them, through blinding tears. I told them how much I loved them, how sorry I was for letting them down. All I could see at that time was a very black tunnel with no light at the end of it, it was as dark as it could be.

I folded up the letters and put them on the breakfast bar. I then very calmly went to the cupboard and took out some tablets and I swallowed as many as I could. All I could hear was the silence of the house, it was almost deafening.

The next thing I remember is waking up in a hospital bed disgusted that I was still alive. I lay there feeling very ill as I tried without success to piece together what had happened. A nurse came to see me and asked if I was okay, I said I felt sick and he said he was not at all surprised, the amount of tablets I had taken I was bound to feel sick. I asked him how I got to the hospital, he said that my husband had come downstairs looking for me and found me lying on the kitchen floor. He called the ambulance and made me sick before they arrived. The nurse said that making me sick saved my life, if my husband had not found me and done what he did I would have died.

I started to cry. I said, 'But don't you see, I wanted to die, I don't want to be here, I have had enough.' The nurse said he was going to get someone to come and talk to me. I told the doctor how I was feeling and she decided that I should stay in hospital for a while. I was feeling so rotten, both physically and emotionally, that I didn't care what happened. I spent three weeks in the hospital, most of the time I just slept. The doctor agreed that I was suffering from exhaustion and there was not much they could do for me, other than let me have a rest, a bit like what a kind relative would do, but as I didn't have any kind relatives, the doctor felt I should stay in hospital for a while.

A day or so into my stay at the hospital, the shame of what I had tried to do hit me. How could I be so selfish to do such a thing? How could I think of leaving my children without their mother? What was I thinking? The children were all I had and I was all they had, how could things have to come to this? I was so worried about the children, but I knew I was no good to them at that time, I needed to get strong again so I could give them my best.

When I returned home three weeks later, I felt a bit better, I felt I could cope again. I thought that London was not the place

CHAPTER 14: SLIPPING

for our four children, I spoke to Damien and told him that I thought we should move to the country, and to my surprise he agreed. But looking back there was no need to move, the children were happy, the one who was not happy was me. I realise now that all the moves we made were just running away from problems, but the problems still came with us.

Chapter 15

Life Alone

In June 2002 we moved to East Anglia, to a beautiful pink five-bedroomed cottage with a white picket fence. It was so pretty, full of character and charm, set in two acres of land so there was plenty of room for the children to run and play. They loved it, they would play outside for hours, making up games, building play houses, it was such a joy to see them all so happy, Aaron and Hope really started to improve, especially my daughter. I had been told that she might never walk or talk, something I refused to believe, and within a year of moving she was walking and talking like any other little girl, although a little behind her age group. I didn't care, I believed that she would catch up when she was ready.

I immersed myself in country life, growing all my own fruit and vegetables and keeping hens. I really got into cooking and loved it so much, and our house became a weekend retreat for my friends in London. I had a blackboard in my kitchen and would write out the menus for the weekend. I enjoyed those weekends with my friends very much.

Things between Damien and I were just okay. I knew that I was falling out of love with him, but I tried very hard to hide that fact. I couldn't help how I felt, every time I looked at him

CHAPTER 15: LIFE ALONE

I remembered what he did to me on our wedding day, and no matter how hard I tried I just couldn't let it go. I got back in to my song writing and guitar playing, which I was enjoying very much. I decided to write some songs and through friends I had met whilst living in the country, I got the opportunity to record an album to raise money for my children's school. It was a wonderful experience and a very happy time.

Busy Bees

> Five little people as busy as bees,
> Five little people all wanting me,
> All trying to be what they want to be,
> My five precious gifts one and all,
> All fighting to be heard, all standing tall.
>
> Listen sweet darlings, I love you each and every one,
> I am so proud of you all and all you have done.
> My five little people as busy as bees,
> Bring so much joy and happiness to me.
> So I thank you my darling little busy bees,
> And make this promise to you,
> Wherever life takes you, and whatever you do,
> I will be here waiting, loving you.

To add to the joy I was experiencing at the time, I received a surprise phone call from my daughter Stephanie. I hadn't seen her for a few years and had thought I would probably never see her again. She asked me if I would like to have her over for her birthday. I nearly died on the spot with excitement, I had only ever seen her for one birthday and the prospect of seeing her on her eighteenth was amazing. She then asked me how would I like to have her come permanently – words cannot describe how I felt when she said she wanted to come and live with me. I had waited seventeen long years to hear her utter those words.

When she arrived I could not believe this beautiful young woman standing in front of me was my baby. I felt like queen bee when I sat around the table and looked at the five beautiful faces of my children, all chatting and laughing together. I was so happy and proud and I felt complete.

Stephanie and I decided to go to London for the weekend. I hadn't been to London in nearly two years and thought I would go and see some of my friends. Damien wasn't too pleased, but he agreed to look after the children. The day I was due to return from London, I received a very nasty phone call from Damien – he was shouting down the phone, calling me the most horrible names, accusing me of having an affair. I couldn't believe what he was saying to me. I told him not to be so ridiculous, but he wouldn't listen. Yes I had friendships, but not affairs. I knew he was very angry and I was not sure what he would do. So Stephanie and I left straight away and headed back home, it was the longest journey ever.

On the way home, I received a call from our local vicar. He told me that Damien had called him to say he was leaving and that he had left the children with a lady in the village. I was in such a state, what on earth was going on? What did Damien think he was doing? I thought I would never get home to see the children. When Stephanie and I arrived at this lady's house,

CHAPTER 15: LIFE ALONE

we were greeted with looks of disapproval, my children were crying, and they told me that Daddy said he was going to get an ice cream, but he never came back.

I gathered up my children and drove home feeling sick about what I would be met with when I got there. My greatest fears were confirmed – Damien was gone, he had cleared out all his stuff, he had taken the business with him, and the office was gone. I didn't know whether to be angry or upset, my children were so distraught. I tried to call him, but true to form he would not answer his phone.

After he left, I began to be bombarded with letters and phone calls from various companies looking for money. Damien as usual had cleared out the bank and I had no money at all. I tried to contact Damien but had no luck. Life was very tough and I had to ring around and try to make some arrangements to pay my bills and the mortgage. We had little or no food, but a dear friend of mine emptied out her cupboards and gave me half of everything she had. The children were missing their dad and couldn't understand why he would not contact them.

But within three months of Damien leaving, things started to settle down a bit. I was managing the bills and was able to keep the house running, and the children were a little less distressed. As a family we had managed to get into a routine and life ticked along okay, and we even managed to have a really good Christmas that year – we laughed and had fun, friends popped in to see us, the house was a lot more relaxed.

On New Year's Eve 2005, I sat watching the celebrations on TV, and as I was watching, an unbelievable sadness swept over me, as images from my life seemed to flash in front of my eyes. I suddenly realised that I had no power over my life. I had let so many people have control over me and cause me great unhappiness. I decided there and then that it was time I took back control, and to do that, I needed to let the past go, I needed to stop hiding from it and pretending it didn't happen. I needed to face it and set that little girl I had kept locked away for all those years free.

The Baby

A baby is born, so the picture says,
It's a picture of me inside my head.
This baby was tortured, hurt and abused,
Neglected, battered, beaten and used.
As I close my eyes, I see myself cry,
This baby forgotten, this baby is I.

I focus a bit harder, and what do I see?
A door in the corner, that's just for me,
With a bright shiny sign saying, Set Yourself Free.
The baby goes silent, a smile on her face,
As she crawls through the door, she's in a safe place.

I sobbed like never before, but my tears were different this time. I wasn't feeling crippled as before, it was the complete opposite, and with every tear I cried, I felt an enormous sense of peace. I went to bed that night feeling exhausted, but calm. The next day I told Stephanie I wanted to go to Ireland. I wanted to go and confront my past and put it behind me once and for all.

CHAPTER 15: LIFE ALONE

We made plans to go to Ireland in February 2006, I was very excited and felt really empowered. I had written lots of poetry and stuck it all up on my kitchen cupboard doors. Every day I would read my poems and feel more empowered. I felt a great presence around me, almost like I had a guardian angel. Although I didn't know much about angels at that time, what I did know was there was definitely a higher power looking after me. I had been given a book called *Feel the Fear and Do It Anyway* and this book opened the doorway for me to start making changes in my life. Although it would take another few years for those changes to happen, I felt I was on the road to creating a better future, free from this crippling pain I was carrying.

A few days before I was due to leave for Ireland, I started to have the strangest emotions. I was in a panic and I would cry uncontrollably as images of my childhood flashed in my mind. My tears were childlike. I decided to keep a diary of how I was feeling, leading up to and during my revisit to the past. It was the first time I had ever kept a diary.

My first entry reads:

23/2/06
It is 24 hours until I board the plane that will take me on a journey back to my childhood. A childhood that was filled with fear, tears, abuse and pain - all these emotions I have carried around with me for 40 years. The purpose of this journey is to face all the pain as a grown woman and to set the little girl inside me free.

Looking back over my diary, I am amazed at the yo-yo emotions I was having – one minute I felt empowered, the next minute I felt so scared I had the feeling that I would surely die on the spot. No matter how I tried to rationalise my fear, it just gripped me in such a way that I had horrendous panic attacks.

I was asked on one occasion, what was the worst part of my childhood. I remember thinking long and hard before giving my answer. I replied, that it would make sense for me to say that it was the abuse, but that was not the case because I didn't know for many years that the abuse was wrong. As I thought more about the question, I became tearful and sad. The worst part of my childhood was fear, I never knew what it was like not to feel fear, and I carried it around with me like a big rucksack on my back. Such was the impact of that fear, I then carried it with me through my adulthood. The journey I was taking was to, once and for all, take this big rucksack of fear off and leave it where it belonged, in the past.

When Stephanie and I arrived in Dublin, we had a lovely evening together. Although I was anxious about the next day, I was determined to have a good time with my daughter and that we did. I had decided to go to Ballymun, as for me that was where some of the worst abuse happened and where I had lost my baby when I was 14 years old.

As we were approaching the flats, I though I was going to be sick, and I thought that my knees would surely buckle underneath me. When we arrived outside the flat, I started to sob almost hysterically, with fear, but also joy. A new regeneration programme was going on in Ballymun, and most of the flats had been boarded up and were ready for demolition. For some reason the only flat boarded up in my street was the

CHAPTER 15: LIFE ALONE

one where I used to live. Every flat still had all its windows, except mine, the wooden boards stuck out like a sore thumb amongst the other panes of glass.

As I looked at my flat, I could see an image of my mother's face looking at me from the kitchen, and as I looked at where my bedroom window would have been I saw an image of my stepfather's face. As I looked I felt so small like a child once more and I cried as one, but as I was crying I started to have an amazing feeling of peace, something I had never experienced before. I looked at the boarded windows and I realised that nothing bad could ever happen again in that flat, and for me that meant an end to the suffering and pain that went on in there. Walking back towards the bus stop I had a feeling of sadness for the little girl I had kept locked up for all those years, I mourned her as I set her free.

When we got back to Dublin city, I suddenly decided I wanted to get some balloons, but where was I going to get them? Dublin was in chaos as a riot had broken out, people were running in panic as hysteria gripped the city. The riot had started as of result of the Orangemen coming down from the North of Ireland who were planning a march down O'Connell Street.

Stephanie and I walked down Henry Street and there happened to be a lady standing on the street with a huge bunch of balloons – she was doing a promotion for a new shop that was to open in Dublin. I asked her if I could have three balloons – two blue ones and a yellow one. I stood in the middle of the street and with tears in my eyes I let a blue balloon go for my mother. I watched it float high in the sky, I stood for a moment and then I said I forgave her for all she had done to me, I wished her peace wherever she was. The second blue balloon I released was for my stepfather. I found it very difficult to do this, but I knew if I wanted to be free I had to do it. As I watched it float away, I said I forgave him for stealing my childhood. The third and final balloon I released, the yellow one, was for me. I asked God and the angels, to help me be a strong woman now, I asked them to free me from the pain I had carried for all these years, I asked them to help me be the best person I could be.

I stood there for what seemed like ages and watched as the three balloons floated higher and higher into the sky. I was crying tears of sadness, sadness that I was saying goodbye to my mother – although she did what she did to me, I loved her desperately and would have done anything for her to love me back. I cried because I felt I was finally letting the evils of my childhood go, and I felt the terrible pain of hurt and rejection starting to leave me. I felt less tormented about what my mother and stepfather had done to me.

When I returned to the UK, I was walking on air. For the first time in my life I felt free, I felt alive. I hadn't been home long when out of the blue I received a call from Damien saying he wanted to meet up to talk. Damien had been gone for eight months without a word or a penny and all of a sudden he wanted to talk. I felt strong enough so I agreed. He told me he was very sorry and wanted to come home. I was not sure I wanted him back, but he promised me that he had changed, he had done a lot of soul-searching and he realised that he wanted me and the children.

I listened to all he had to say and a big part of me really wanted to believe him. I really wanted my children to have their dad, I really wanted to be a complete family. I believed that I

CHAPTER 15: LIFE ALONE

was strong enough to make our family work, so I agreed to Damien coming home, but made it clear that under no circumstances would I tolerate any more abuse. He promised me so faithfully that he would not hurt a hair on my head. When would I ever learn?

Within a short time, it all started again. This time I was a little less scared of him and would try to stand up for myself when he criticised me, or belittled me, but nothing prepared me for the outburst that was to come a couple of weeks later.

My Ring

I look at the ring on my left hand, twisted and mangled like my heart,
The diamond on top used to sparkle and shine, just like the outside of me,
Inside I'm dented, just like my ring, but I used to sparkle, smile and sing,
My old ring and I have been through the wringer.

I gaze at myself in the bathroom mirror, I cry and I ask, what went wrong?
I see my sparkle has completely gone.
I, like my ring, was pretty and bright, perfectly formed, perfectly right,
With a few rough edges like the diamond inset, I gaze in the mirror and I think…
Is it over yet?

Chapter 16

Back to Ireland

Damien had been making his own home brewed beer and was drinking on this particular evening. He started to do what he had always done, telling me how inadequate and how useless I was at looking after the house and children. I was so sick of hearing it, no matter how I explained how difficult it was looking after two children with special needs, as well as the other children, and without any help, he wouldn't listen. The more I tried to explain, the angrier he got, the more frustrated I got. Suddenly he jumped out of his chair and went upstairs and called Stephanie and Josh – he told them to come downstairs as he was going to kill their mother. Before I knew what was happening Damien had grabbed a knife and was holding it to my throat, saying 'I'm going to kill her, I'm going to kill her.' Josh got angry and he grabbed the knife out of his father's hand and put it on the work-top. Damien very drunkenly, picked it up again and, waving it at all of us, told us if we came near him he would kill us all. Josh quickly grabbed the phone and called the police. Damien dropped the knife and ran out of the house.

The police arrived and had their dogs out looking for Damien. I was distraught as were Stephanie and Josh. We gave statements and the police told us that when they found Damien

CHAPTER 16: BACK TO IRELAND

he would be arrested and taken away. The police dogs found him hiding in a field, and the next day I got a call to go and pick Damien up from the police station. It was a very silent journey home, as I once again wrestled with what to do. Here I was again, scared. Thoughts ran through my head at a hundred miles an hour: what about the children, they love their dad, how can I remove him from their lives again? The fights were not aimed at them, but having them see what was going on was wrong. I just did not know what to do.

I could feel myself slipping again and the important journey I'd made to Ireland was now a distant memory. All my positive poetry that I had on my cupboards was gone, Damien took it all down. The feeling I was fooling myself in believing life would be any different was as strong as it had ever been. So I did what I had always done, put my head in the sand and pretended it wasn't happening. That back pack I had left behind on my journey returned, only this time it was heavier.

My relationship with Stephanie became strained, we started to argue a lot usually over boys, and after one bad argument she packed her bags and was gone. I was devastated. Although I knew things could not continue as they were and it was right for her to leave at that time, it broke my heart. I tried to call her to make amends, but sadly to this day I have not seen or heard from her, despite several attempts.

I soon became very ill with all the stress, and I was rushed to hospital suffering with pleurisy. I was so ill I really thought I wouldn't make it. I spent a week in the hospital and was then allowed home under the strict instructions that I rested. But that was not going to happen in my house. Damien came and collected me from the hospital, but when we got home he dropped me at the front door and said he was going back to work. There was no cup of tea, no hug, no nothing. I went into the house still feeling most unwell, but I just had to get on and do things as if I had never been sick. I then developed post-viral syndrome which almost paralysed me for a whole year.

Having been so ill, I decided I wanted to go back to Ireland. I believed that we could have a better life there, we would be able to buy a house without a mortgage, and the children would have all of Damien's family around them. I truly believed going back to Ireland was the best thing for all of us. But again it was just running away.

Within six weeks of putting our house on the market it was sold, and for more than we could have imagined, giving us enough to buy a nice house in Ireland with some money left over, taking some of the pressure off. The children were excited about the move, although sad to leave their friends. I decided to stay in London with the children for a few days to make sure that all went well with the move, I didn't want to take the children over and not have the house secured. We had a lovely time. I found it hard to say goodbye to my friends, but I totally believed that this was a whole new start for the family.

The children and I flew to Dublin and were met by Damien. As we came through immigration and I saw him standing there, for the first time in our married life I looked at him and realised for sure that I definitely didn't love him any more. I felt panicked and sad, sad because it was true, panicked because I didn't know what to do. I felt a huge responsibility for taking the decision to move everyone over to Ireland, and I felt I really had to put my feelings aside and concentrate on making things work.

CHAPTER 16: BACK TO IRELAND

Home

Don't be angry my sweet loving child,
Let go of the anger you hold deep inside.
You're home now, you're safe here with me,
Kick off your chains, set yourself free.
Stop beating yourself up, stop being scared,
See a bright future, your voice will be heard.
I know you've been hurt and the pain runs deep,
I know at night you sometimes don't sleep,
But listen sweet darling, those days are gone.
Give yourself time, you'll blossom, you're strong.
You're home now sweet darling, all will be grand,
Whenever you need me, reach out, hold my hand.

When we arrived at the new house, it was the first time I had seen it properly. I had only seen pictures of it on the internet. It was much bigger that I had realised and it was a very beautiful house, with large electric gates. Josh very excitedly showed me around and remarked that I was not showing any excitement. I smiled at him and said I was excited, I was just feeling a little tired, but inside I wasn't sure if I had made the right decision about moving over. Within a few weeks we were moved in and unpacked in our new home. The children had started new schools, but were struggling a little with being teased for having an English accent. Many times they would come home crying and they were missing their friends from England. Damien hated Ireland and constantly blamed me for the unhappiness the children were experiencing. I tried to keep positive and believed that these hiccups were only temporary, everyone struggles when they do such a big move.

Sure enough the children did settle and make friends, but Damien's barrage of abuse did not stop. Sometimes it would get so bad that I would get in my car and drive to the lake, and I would sit in my car just feeling so desperate, so lonely and still feeling so trapped. The continuous criticism and verbal abuse from Damien was grinding me down, and coupled with not having a support network of my own, I could feel myself retreating again, I could feel myself becoming really withdrawn.

Making friends was proving harder than I had imagined. Ireland was not as I had remembered it from twenty years before, and of course in that time I had changed too. I decided I was not going to go into that dark tunnel again. Then I met a woman who introduced me to angel cards, her sense of positivity and belief was so inspiring to me, and we would chat for ages. She spoke about the universe and believed that what you gave out, was what you received back. For me this was a bit difficult to believe, I mean what had I given out to the universe to deserve all the abuse I had and was still suffering? What had I given out to the universe as a child to deserve what my mother and stepfather had done to me? There was no answer to those questions, only a suggestion to put my faith in the angels and they would guide me to the changes I needed to make, they would protect me and all that was important to me.

I came home after my first visit armed with a book on angels. I got the kids sorted, Damien came in and did his usual barrage of

CHAPTER 16: BACK TO IRELAND

abuse, then stormed out to the pub. Our move to Ireland had made it easier for Damien to indulge in his love of alcohol, as we lived within walking distance of nine pubs, so he had his pick. Sometimes he wouldn't come home until the early hours of the morning.

This particular evening, I sat in the silence of the kitchen and began to read the angel book. As I was reading I could feel a real sense of peace in my heart, and I decided to pray and call my angels around me. I felt a gentle breeze pass me and the most amazing scent of a perfume I had never smelt before. I felt like I was being protected, like two big arms were holding me, and I felt for that moment all my fears and anxieties were being slowly taken away. Although the whole experience only lasted for a few moments, it was an experience that I will never forget.

I became very interested in the power of prayer, and the power of a higher being. I read as much as I could and spoke to as many people as I could who shared the same interest. What I learnt from this was that we all have the power to change our lives. For me, that was the start of the life-changing decisions I would make. Every day I would pray, I would ask my higher power to help and guide me through each day, and although things at home were pretty bad, somehow I didn't feel as if I was alone anymore.

I decided to record and release a Christmas song I had written in a bid to raise enough money to buy a much-needed minibus for a school for children with special needs. I also wanted to highlight the difficulties faced by children with autism. I gathered fifty children from six local schools and with the help of a dear friend, spent eleven months training these children to sing. It was a wonderful project to work on, so many people were generous with their time and talents, they believed in what I was doing and supported me fully.

Every Saturday morning we rehearsed in the village hall, and most Saturdays I would be almost on my knees. Damien hated what I was doing, and would deliberately start a row on Friday night totally demoralising and frightening me. I would question my very existence. I knew what he was trying to do to me, he wanted to see me crumble and fail, but there was no way I was going to let him succeed. So I thought, but I was crumbling.

Despite all the heartache at home nothing could take away the joy I was experiencing on this project. Damien and I were drifting further and further apart and the fights were becoming more frequent. When I came home after rehearsals on Saturday, I would feel a great sadness at just how bad things were between Damien and I. I knew we were definitely over this time, but I didn't know how I was going to get out of this marriage, and I knew that Damien wouldn't let me go.

The weight of this deep unhappiness and the constant verbal and emotional abuse and control from Damien, started to grind me down, so that some days I couldn't get out of bed. I put on a lot of weight hoping that Damien would find me repulsive and would leave me alone, but the threat of him wanting what he felt he should have was never far away. I couldn't bear this terrible unhappiness I was going through. I knew I was living a lie – from the outside we looked like the perfect family, a big house, a successful business, beautiful children. Not one person knew what was going on. I would paint on a smile and hold my head high as soon as I walked out of the door, and every day I prayed for strength. I produced two very successful amateur dramatic shows, that sold out to full houses around Ireland, and I was regularly asked to do radio debates – I became a performer worthy of an Oscar for hiding this terrible heartache I was feeling.

CHAPTER 16: BACK TO IRELAND

As soon as I would pull up the driveway of our house, that sick heavy feeling of desperation gripped me in such a way that I found it almost impossible to function normally. I would lock myself away in my bedroom, lost in this world of desperate entrapment, filled with unhappiness. I would pray and meditate every single day, and it was the strength I gained from that that helped push me along to the life changes I needed to make. Although I was not aware of it at the time, I just knew that in amongst the turmoil I was going through, every now and again I would get an amazing feeling of strength, a feeling that this pain was going to come to an end soon.

It wouldn't be until Christmas 2010, as I was putting up the decorations, that I would get what I can only describe as a strong message from my inner voice that this would be the last Christmas I would spend in the family home. I would regularly get little messages but such was my fear, I couldn't imagine that what I desperately longed for could actually happen for me. Looking back, I now know what I didn't realise at the time – I was being carried along gently on the crest of a wave and I had nothing to fear, I was being totally protected by my higher being.

In February 2008 an opportunity had arisen for me to go to Canada with my best friend for three weeks. I knew at that time, if I didn't get a break I was going to crumble completely. Despite the angry reaction from Damien and the guilt he was piling on me, I decided I had to go. I flew to London first to meet up with my friend, and I arrived in what can only be described as a terrible mess. I was distraught, dishevelled and was having the most horrendous panic attacks. My friend met me at the airport, she put her arms around me, and I nearly collapsed I was sobbing so much. When we got to her apartment we went through my suitcase and both had a good laugh at what I had packed, there was nothing of any use at all, I had packed shoes that didn't match. Everything about my suitcase showed the state I was in when I left.

When we arrived in Canada I found the size of the country overwhelming. I was like a child with excitement. We stayed with my friend's sister, and what struck me was the closeness of the family. Although everyone was speaking French as we were in New Brunswick, the love and respect they had for each other shone through like a bright star. I couldn't help feeling a little jealous of their closeness, I realised how damaged and fractured my family was and I felt very sad. I was welcomed into their family so warmly and enjoyed every moment of it. I used my time in Canada to pray and to write. My friend was a tower of strength to me and encouraged me so much.

Every day I would call home to speak to the children. Damien always answered the phone, he was always so cold and horrid to me, making me feel guilty for going away, and he never had anything nice or warm to say. It upset me until I would hear the beautiful sweet voices of my children, telling me their little tales and oozing love to me down the phone. I missed them dreadfully, but knew I needed this break. My time in Canada helped me to get strong again. I lost some weight and hated myself a little less. I made the decision that I was going to write as much as I could, and I started to write a film script, a comedy drama. I found writing took me into another world, a world that was happy and full of laughter. When I was writing I forgot everything, time seemed to pass and I didn't notice all my pain and sadness – it seemed to disappear for those hours I was lost in my characters.

CHAPTER 16: BACK TO IRELAND

When the time came for us to return home, I was ready. I was ready to deal with whatever I was met with when I returned. Damien met me from the airport with a frosty reception, but I didn't expect anything more from him. We drove home in silence, all I wanted was to see my children. When I got home the house was a complete mess, but the children were happy and as far as I was concerned that was all that mattered, I had the rest of my life to clean the house. I had a lovely afternoon with the children sharing stories of our time apart. I was feeling so much stronger and Damien's behaviour towards me didn't seem to bother me as much. I continued with my writing and it became my saving grace, it was only when I got seriously in to writing did I realise that if it were not for that I probably would never have got through all the things that happened to me when I was a child.

Christmas Eve 2009 finally made me realise that it was time I took steps to sort my life out once and for all, although it would take me another eighteen months to make those changes. I was busy preparing for Christmas Day. Damien came home from doing his Christmas visits to his family, he started to drink quite heavily, but I chose to ignore it, enjoying the excitement of my younger children as they discussed and prepared their treats for Santa Claus and his reindeer. Josh, who was now 20, had some of his friends around, which was quite normal in our house. Our house was an open house for my children's friends. We had a music room at the side of the house and my two sons being musicians would gather their friends and they would all rehearse. I loved having them around. They were all great kids, and I enjoyed hearing their stories and listening to the banter between them. They were like a breath of fresh air.

As the evening got later, I noticed that Damien had got very drunk. I was not pleased at all, but continued with my evening getting my younger children to bed. When I came back downstairs Damien had gathered Josh and his friends around and he was proudly telling them about his drug-fueled days in London. The boys were hanging on every word he said and the more interest they took, the more Damien told them. I noticed that my son and his friends kept disappearing upstairs for a few minutes before returning to the kitchen. For a while I didn't catch on to what was happening, then the penny dropped, I got that sick panic feeling again, the one I got when I knew Damien had done something.

Oh my God, they were taking drugs. I didn't know what to do. I tried to busy myself while being invisible to everyone else in the room. When the lads had heard enough of Damien's stories they went in to the front room to watch TV. Damien was still sitting in the kitchen, a self-satisfied drunken grin on his face. I looked at the clock and it was almost midnight. I still had a few things to do, so I went into the living room and asked my son's friends if they could go home now as it was late. The boys with no complaint all apologised and left.

I was just about to start sorting out the presents for the following morning, when Josh turned on me, angry that I had asked his friends to leave. I turned to him and told him he had no right to bring drugs into our house and I asked him if he had not learnt anything from what I had been through with his father. At this point Damien started to mock me, saying the most terrible things to me, and Josh joined in. My son had that same look in his eyes as I had seen many times with his father. As the barrage of abuse continued, Damien stood to one side,

CHAPTER 16: BACK TO IRELAND

his hands in his pockets and an evil grin on his face. My heart was breaking, this was my son, how could he speak to me as he was? Josh picked up a kitchen chair and threw it at me. I ran out of the house and got into my car just knowing I had to get away, but I couldn't. The electric gates needed a remote to operate them and only Damien had the zapper, he wouldn't allow me to have one. This was his way of keeping me in the house.

I drove my car right up to the gates and just sobbed, I sobbed and wailed with this terrible pain in my heart. What was I to do? How could my beautiful son speak to me like that? How had I not noticed that he was smoking cannabis? How could his father stand there and laugh as this all happened? I cannot describe the level of pain I felt that night. All I knew was that it was Christmas Eve and my little darlings would wake up looking for Santa. I finally fell asleep for a short while.

When I woke up it was still dark and I was frozen cold. I crept back into the house, my eyes almost stuck together from crying. The house was silent, fairy lights twinkled everywhere and there was the smell of food cooking – it made what had happened that evening seem like a bad dream, like it never happened, but it did. Through tears, I finished getting my children's parcels sorted, I made a cup of tea and I sat in silence feeling more trapped than ever before with a desperate desire to do something, but what? As I sat there, I prayed and prayed.

An hour or so after I had come back into the house, I heard the patter of little feet on the stairs. I hid in the kitchen and listened to the gasps of excitement as the children opened the living room door. They came bursting into the kitchen, and seeing me, excitedly told me Santa had come. I pretended to be surprised and they led me into the front room to show me all their presents. I sat and watched as one by one they opened them, squealing with delight at every one they unwrapped. I sat and played with them for a while, trying not to show my broken heart. Damien and Josh never stirred, all I could hear was the heavy snoring of Damien booming down the stairs.

As dinnertime approached, Damien appeared looking worse for wear. The children excitedly showed him what Santa had brought for them, but Damien didn't want to know, telling them that he was not feeling well and he would look at their toys later. I didn't say a word to him – I thought, this day is for the children and I am not going to let anything or anyone upset it. As I was laying the table Josh came to me also looking worse for wear. Very uncomfortably he told me to forget last night, it was Christmas so let's enjoy it. I agreed, yes it was Christmas but I would speak to him later in the week about last night. Christmas went off okay, the children were happy, but for me I felt completely dead inside.

I talked to Josh a few days later and told him that I would not tolerate that behaviour from him. I told him I was his mother and I deserved respect, he agreed and promised it wouldn't happen again. I really wanted to believe him, but somehow I doubted it. That Christmas Eve I had seen the same fire in his eyes as I had seen many times before in his father.

On New Year's Eve we were invited to a friend's house and I was introduced to his nephew who was a writer and director. I was so delighted to meet him, I started to tell him about my writing and I could not believe how interested he was. He asked if I could come over a couple of days later and show him what I had written. This I happily did and he said he liked it! I

CHAPTER 16: BACK TO IRELAND

couldn't believe my ears, I had been writing from such a young age, but had never dreamt of showing anyone my writing because I never thought I was good enough. My new director friend taught me step-by-step how to write a good film script and we worked closely together on getting a script finished.

Doing that took my busy mind away from what was happening at home with Damien. His unrelenting desire to see me crushed was always present. It was like he had a verbal pickaxe and kept chipping away at me until I would get to the point where I was doubting my very existence again. I would somehow crawl back to life and function again, this yo-yo effect went on almost daily, and some days I didn't want to get out of bed at all.

In bed I would think of ways to get out of this nightmare and I would pray so hard. What was I to do? I had no money, no family, nothing. I had invested almost 25 years in this relationship and I had no financial security at all and no one I could turn to. Damien controlled everything and didn't want me to have anything at all. By chance one day I had found a letter from his life insurance company and I jokingly asked him if he had cancelled his policy. As quick as anything he snatched the letter out of my hand. He had that 'I just got found out' look on his face. My heart sank, that was money for the children. He said he wanted to make sure I didn't have one penny from him. How low would this man go to see me destroyed? He would never have told me there was no life insurance – I would have found out the hard way.

Now Damien started to affect my relationship with the children. If I got cross with them over their messy rooms, or the way they spoke to me, or indeed anything, Damien would shout at me to leave them alone, and he would encourage them to answer me back in a very disrespectful way. I felt as if my house had become a war zone and I was the target, if I said anything about anything I would be verbally attacked. No matter how I approached things, I was always in the firing line.

My Family

My family, my one true love, my every breath,
It's all so broken, like it's dying a death,
This unit I fought so hard to keep strong,
Is now so damaged, it's all gone wrong.

Violence, abuse, it's all taken its toll,
The children take on the abuser's role.
Gone is the love, respect and laughter,
Replaced with hatred, hurt and anger.

These beautiful babies that I bore,
That I raised, I love and adore,
Are broken souls and so confused,
They don't understand how I was used,
They don't understand how I was abused.

It became part of their everyday life,
To see a mum scream as their dad beat his wife.
My family is damaged, it's all so broken,
Now only words of hate are spoken.

CHAPTER 16: BACK TO IRELAND

Things had become so bad, that I felt I had given up. I locked myself away, making excuses to the few friends I had as to why I couldn't see them. I became almost like a recluse, nothing interested me, nothing stimulated me, I became a totally different person. Gone was the smiling get-up-and-go girl; gone was the girl who, no matter how bad things were would always manage to find a way to pull through; gone was my very identity, and I didn't care anymore. I was slipping into a space that I had never been in before, where I had totally given up. The desperation from, and realisation of, the abuse I had and was suffering took over my very being. I didn't know what was right or what was wrong anymore. No matter how I prayed I couldn't seem to pull myself out of this horrible space.

I had tried to speak to Damien many times about us separating, but he would not discuss it. All I felt was a deep guilt for being so unhappy, and a terrible overwhelming feeling that I was stuck in this toxic violent marriage for ever. Damien was just getting stronger and I was getting weaker.

He spent a lot of time in the village, being the pillar of the community, and getting involved in all sorts of events. When he returned home, the power and control would ooze out of him like he was a big black panther. I had become a panicking, shivering, reclusive wreck and Damien thrived on it. The children had become disrespectful towards me and angry. If I said no, they would go to Damien and he would say yes, undermining my ability as a mother. No matter what I said to the children he would contradict me, and things got so bad that the children stopped asking me anything and went straight to their father. I felt they had lost respect for me because of who I had become. I felt I had lost all the skills I had developed throughout my life. I questioned everything I did, working myself into such a state that I eventually convinced myself and wholeheartedly believed that I was a terrible person and that everything that had happened to me was my fault. I had felt down before, I had felt desperate before, but I had never felt like this.

Chapter 17

Fighting Back

I used to often hear an advert on the radio for the local domestic violence unit. Somehow every time I heard it, it used to upset me – deep down I knew I needed their help, but I felt if I went to them, I would be openly admitting that I was being abused. I didn't think I had the skills even to do that. Where would I start? I had hidden it all for forty-four years. How could I now go to a stranger and tell them exactly what had happened to me for all these years?

Then one day having prayed so hard, somewhere deep inside me I got the courage to pick up the phone. A soft voice said hello, and I started to cry uncontrollably. Through my tears I said, 'Hello my name is Cassie, I am suffering domestic violence and have done for almost twenty-five years, and I need some help.' I talked for what seemed like ages. As I tried to explain what was happening and what had happened, I felt tongue-tied. I found it so hard to put into words, I had kept everything to myself for all those years, I had pretended and lived in denial of just how bad things were for all of my life. How was I ever going to be able to get all that stuff in my head out?

The lady on the other end of the phone was so gentle and patient with me, and she made an appointment for me to go and see her. When I came off the phone, I felt really scared, but I knew it was something I had to do. My life was in tatters and I needed somehow to try and take control of it again.

As soon as I started attending the domestic violence unit, I started to take back control over my life. I realised that I could do things for myself and I was not this person who could do nothing, at last I could see a way out. I went to the domestic violence unit for many months. I had one-to-one sessions with a lovely lady there, but for the first few visits I found it difficult to put into words the abuse I had suffered, it was like I was speaking about someone else's life, not mine.

During one session, we worked with a template on which was a circle with lots of writing on it. The lady explained in great detail that the circle represented the circle of domestic violence. As she patiently went through it with me, I saw that she was describing my life in great detail. I became upset: I had lived my whole life not knowing what was abuse and what wasn't; I had lived my whole life not knowing what was acceptable and what wasn't; I had lived my whole life feeling responsible for everything that had happened; I had lived my whole life believing that everything was my fault, and here in front of me was the proof that not one moment of what happened was my fault. Here in front of me was the proof that no one, but no one, deserves to be abused under any circumstances and what I was suffering and had suffered was abuse of the highest degree.

This realisation had a huge impact on me, I slowly started to comprehend just how horrific and traumatic my life had been. This sent me into a spiralling round of panic attacks. How had I allowed all this to happen? How had I not known that it was wrong? How could I have been so stupid and allowed so many

CHAPTER 17: FIGHTING BACK

people to have complete control over my life? All these questions and more flooded my mind. I knew that I really had to do something.

The Phoenix

Watch the phoenix as she rises out of the ashes,
She flaps her wings and tries to fly,
Her wings are broken, she starts to cry.

She lifts her head, feels the sun beaming down,
She flaps her wings, and begins to groan.
The pain is so bad, it's restricting her flight,
She is desperate to fly from darkness to light.
She takes a deep breath to control the pain,
She flaps her wings and tries again.

She is up she is gliding, though her wings are sore,
She is enjoying the freedom, she wants more,
She flaps her wings with all her strength,
She's nearly there but her wings are bent.

Up she soars, tears of joy down her face,
New found freedom she will embrace,
Her wings get stronger, she is full of glee,
She is happy not frightened, now she is free.

My visits to the domestic violence unit were the best thing I have ever done. I learnt so much about myself during those sessions and I also learnt a lot about the boundaries of abuse. I could feel myself getting stronger every day with the realisation that I did not have to put up with this any more. I realised that I did have the power within to make the changes I needed in my life. Coupled with the strength I was feeling, was a huge fear, a fear of not being able to stand on my own two feet. Being told for so many years how useless and incompetent I was, exacerbated this fear. But with the support of the domestic violence unit, I began to make changes in the life I was living.

I made the decision that I had to get out of this relationship, but I knew Damien would never leave the family home. It was suggested that I make an application to the courts to get a protection order which would mean that Damien could not be abusive to me in any way physically or mentally, but by that time I was so scared. I could not get anyone to understand the fear I was feeling or the control that Damien had over me. I couldn't get anyone to understand how manipulating and clever Damien was. I knew that if I were to get to a protection order out whilst I was still living in the house, he would have made my life even more hellish than it already was, and I was afraid I would crash completely.

I made the painful decision to leave the family home myself for my own sanity and protection. With support from the domestic violence unit and my GP I was able to secure a house and a small weekly allowance from social security. Once I had done this I thought that I was confident enough to deal with Damien. I sat him down and told him I was leaving. I told him that I really wanted him to be fair and to respect my decision

CHAPTER 17: FIGHTING BACK

and to make this final break-up as amicable as possible for the sake of our children. Damien went mad, he started calling me horrendous names and told me in no uncertain terms that I was not taking the children, nor was I going to take anything from the house. I got very upset and begged him to be reasonable – the house I was renting was only a couple of miles down the road, the children could go between the two houses and it was up to us to be seen to be getting on for their sake – but my pleas fell on deaf ears. I spoke to Lizzy, Hope and Aaron, I told them I was leaving and that I wanted them to come with me. Aaron said he would stay with Damien, but that he would come and visit me regularly. Lizzy and Hope said they were coming with me. I felt Josh was an adult and could make up his own mind, he had been through enough and that I didn't need to involve him. Although Aaron had made the decision to stay and I was heartbroken, I knew that he would be fine.

I knew, difficult and as bullish as Damien could be, and as strong as I thought I was and as much as I thought I could handle him, nothing prepared me for what he would actually do.

I was still continuing my sessions at the domestic violence unit and I am sure if it wasn't for that I surely would have crumbled. I started keeping a diary of events leading up to my departure, and reading back over it now makes for terrifying, sad and desperate reading. Once I had sorted out the children each night, I would take myself up to bed at about 7 p.m. just to keep out of Damien's way. It was like having a monster in the house and I was really frightened of him. One of my entries read:

THURSDAY
Been given the silent treatment all day, was skulking around trying to keep out of Damien's way, the atmosphere is so tense its breaking my heart. Why does he have to be so nasty? He has been hovering outside my bedroom door, I am so frightened. I went downstairs to get a drink and he started taunting me for sex, he was very intimidating, when will it end???

Another entry:

MONDAY
Had a lot of running around to do today, Damien didn't come home last night so at least I had peace. I tried to call him to ask him to take care of the children because I had to go to Dublin to have a check on a lump I have on my breast. I am a little worried about the lump but with everything that's going on I haven't had any time to think about it. Damien sent me some vile messages, he refused to have the children and wouldn't give me the petrol money to go to the hospital in Dublin. I had to ask Bridie and Patrick to help me out. When I got to the hospital I got the all clear, the lump I had was a cyst, thank God, at least that's something I don't have to deal with.

CHAPTER 17: FIGHTING BACK

This went on for a further week, but what was to blow my world apart was Lizzy telling me she would not come with me. One evening I was telling her off for being cheeky to me, when Damien started to shout at me in front of her telling me what a disaster I was and how dare I tell his princess off. He started to mock and jeer at me, as my daughter watched. To my horror she then started shouting at me calling me names, as her father sat smilingly encouraging her. I was devastated, here was my little girl looking with pure hate at me whilst her father looked on with joy and amusement. I tried to calm Lizzy down, but she didn't want me near her, she screamed at me that she wasn't going to live with me she was staying with her dad.

I was totally heartbroken. The next day I tried to talk to her, but she was still very angry and spoke to me in a way she had never done before. Damien said, 'See, not even your own kids want you, you have pushed everyone away and will end up a sad lonely old woman.'

I felt crushed, only Hope was coming with me. As I tried to pack, Damien followed me around the house taking things away from me. I ended up with seven small boxes of belongings. How did it come to this? As I looked at the boxes in my car I thought, 'Is that all I have after forty-four years, seven little boxes?' As I drove away, I thought my heart would break in two for sure. When I pulled up at the new house I had mixed emotions – on one hand I felt relieved that I had finally got away from Damien, and on the other hand I was so scared and heartbroken: scared for the future, heartbroken for my other children. But somewhere amongst all those emotions was the true belief that I had done the right thing.

The first night in our new house was very strange. My daughter was a little nervous and upset, and asked if she could sleep with me. As she cuddled up with me and fell asleep, I looked at her, I looked at how beautiful she was, how perfect she was, just like all my children. I felt a crippling ache in my heart for my other children, but thought I have to be strong and hold on to the belief that they will come to me. I fell into a deep sleep and slept as I had hadn't done in what seemed like years.

The next morning as I lay there with Hope sleeping next to me, I knew that I had definitely done the right thing. I came downstairs, it was a beautiful sunny morning, and I made a cup of tea feeling a great sense of peace. I looked out of the window and couldn't help but laugh, there were no gates, I wasn't trapped anymore. Almost everywhere I had lived with Damien had gates. He would lock them in the evenings and only he had a key, this used to make me feel even more trapped than I already was. But here I was in my new house, not frightened, not worried about Damien walking in. I felt a wonderful feeling of freedom.

My daughter and I made our house into a home and although the heartache of not having my other children with me was never far away, I for the first time in my life was actually free. I was sleeping like I had never slept before and I realised I could stand on my own two feet, and all those things Damien used to say to me, all the times he told me I was useless and convinced me I couldn't live without him were all lies, I was more than capable of doing anything I wanted to do. It was wonderful. Every day I would pray and thank God for what I had. I started to do small meditations every morning and was feeling strong and peaceful. Hope and I got into a routine, and

CHAPTER 17: FIGHTING BACK

although we had very little money, we didn't go without and I was managing the bills okay.

Damien kept sending me horrible threatening text messages, which frightened me because he was able to tell me when I was home and when I wasn't. If I was in the garden I would see his car slowly driving past the house, and it put the fear of God into me. I begged Damien to stop, I begged him to open positive dialogue with me for the sake of the children, but he wouldn't do it. I was missing my other children dreadfully. I went round to the house to see them, but Damien had changed the combination on the gates and I couldn't get into the house. I called him to let me in, but as usual he wouldn't answer his phone. I decided that I had to be strong as Damien was not going to cooperate. He told me that he would feel happiness when he saw me living in a cardboard box with nothing, because I was nothing and that was where I belonged.

I went to a government agency for help, and pleaded with them to help me get Lizzy back. I was completely shocked when the lady I was talking to took out a file with my name all over it. She proceeded to tell me that Damien had been in touch with them for the past four years, making some serious allegations against me. I can't explain how I felt as she read out some of the allegations – Damien had told them I wasn't fit to look after a dog, never mind a family and he had said I was an alcoholic. I attended a drugs clinic to prove I was not an alcoholic, and the woman there agreed I drank no more than anyone else in my situation. I asked the lady why on earth had someone not contacted me over these four years to ask me what was going on? The woman told me Damien had asked them not to contact me, as he was only making them aware of the situation. But the situation Damien had spoken of was nothing more than a pack of lies.

I was absolutely soul destroyed, how could he have been so nasty to tell so many lies about me? I very clearly told the woman what really had happened and why I had to leave my family home. But I felt my words were useless. I went to as many people as possible to try and get some help to get my children back, but wherever I turned I was met with a very negative response.

I was also trying to communicate with my children, but Damien had told them so many lies about me that they did not want to speak to me. Even though it was heartbreaking I knew it wasn't their fault, they were all so confused with the poison Damien was feeding them. Hope was missing the rest of the family very much, but Damien had made no effort to see her. When she called him he would either not answer his phone, or make an excuse not to see her. This went on for a few weeks.

In the meantime Damien had engaged a solicitor. He denied all the abuse and said I was the cause of the marriage breakdown. The day came when I had to go to court and I thought I would at last get my voice heard. I went armed with police reports from the UK, my diaries, the support of the domestic violence unit, and the drugs unit. Two dear friends of mine had also come to give me support.

As I sat there with my stomach in knots, I saw Damien appear with Lizzy. I started to cry, nobody in my party could believe that he had taken our daughter out of school and brought her to court with him. This was between me and Damien, how could he do such a thing? How could he use our daughter to hide behind? My solicitor came and told me that Damien had brought Lizzy to court to testify against me. I looked down the

CHAPTER 17: FIGHTING BACK

corridor at Damien who was laughing and joking. I saw the beautiful frame of my daughter and I felt like I could die with the pain in my heart. I decided that there was no way I could stand in court and listen to her repeat all the lies Damien had told her. For her sake and mine, I agreed not to go into court. I didn't get the opportunity to put my case across, I didn't get a chance to speak one word. My heart was in pieces, was there nothing that this man would stop at to destroy me?

Over the next few months things went from bad to worse. I had to finally accept that there was no one to help me and there was no way I was going to get the justice I deserved. I also had to accept that my children were not going to come and live with me, which was truly heartbreaking.

I plodded on for a few more months trying to get work, but unsuccessfully. Some days the pain of not having my children with me would grip me so hard that I would sit on the floor with the most horrendous pains running through me as I sobbed and sobbed, knowing that there was nothing I could do. I was also experiencing terrible flashbacks and nightmares. The reality of my life of abuse hit me very hard and some times sent me into what I can only describe as shock. I was constantly asking myself 'Oh my God, how did that happen?' For many months I went through a lot of 'Oh my Gods'.

Damien was still giving me a hard time, he would drive up and down the road outside my house terrifying the life out of me. If I went shopping I would constantly be looking over my shoulder, if I was out and I saw his car I would have a panic attack. No matter how I tried to tell myself that Damien could not hurt me anymore, his very presence still felt like he was controlling me. I just knew I was not far enough away from him, in order for me to have any quality of life I had to get as far away from him as I could.

Then an offer to go to London came my way through a friend. I thought long and hard about what to do. I wrestled with the decision I would have to make. Damien had made death threats and part of me believed that anything was possible with him. I had never left him before and he was still very angry. Even though there were days I was almost on my knees with the fear he had put into me, and with the loss of my children, he didn't know I was frightened, he didn't know I was spending a lot of time in tears. From the outside, I looked like I was fully in control, and it was my meditation and angel cards that gave me the strength to get through each day.

I decided that going to London was the right thing to do. I had spent over half my life there so it wasn't like I was going somewhere I didn't know. I talked to Hope about going, and although she was apprehensive she said she wanted to come. I asked my other children to come with me, but they all refused saying they didn't want anything to do with me. I started to wrestle with myself again, was I really doing the right thing? I had spent almost a year living in that house with just my youngest daughter. I had tried and tried to open communication with Damien regarding the children. I had tried on hundreds of occasions to talk to my children but no matter what I did I was not making any progress. So I packed up and prepared to head to London. I got the relevant permission needed from the court to take my daughter out of the country. Much to my surprise Damien agreed so we were all set to go. I secured a school place for Hope, and we had somewhere to stay. Everything was looking good.

CHAPTER 17: FIGHTING BACK

A few days before we were due to leave, Hope decided she wanted to spend Christmas with her father, promising me that she would join me in London in time for school. I was very reluctant to let her, but felt I had to listen to what she wanted and I agreed. I asked Damien to please cooperate and promise that he would send her to me after Christmas, and he promised faithfully that he would, saying he knew that our daughter wanted to be with me. I trusted his words and I allowed her to go. Damien came to collect her, but he wouldn't even look at me. As I watched Hope excitedly gather her things together, I asked him to please keep the promise he had made. I saw that nasty grin on his face, the one I had seen so many times when he was planning and scheming. I tried to ignore it as I helped my daughter with her things, she threw her arms around my neck and told me how much she loved me and that she would see me soon. But something inside told me I had made a terrible mistake, and I was to be proved right.

The Last Call of the Black Panther

The Black Panther bellows his last scary roar, as he takes my baby away,
I'm laid broken and crushed on the kitchen floor.
Inside I am screaming 'please let her go'
'Don't take my baby' I silently say,
But he snarls and he grins as he takes her away,
'I love you mummy' my baby says.

The pain in my heart, it's hurting, it's sore,
As the last sound I hear is the slam of the door,
The silence is deafening, as my heart breaks in two,
Crushed I still lay there – what do I do?
Flashes of laughter, hugs, smiles and tears,
Of my beautiful children I had for those years.

But all has been taken away from me now,
By the panther, the abuser, the wife-beater, the user.
I pick myself up, I walk around the house, empty rooms, so still so silent.
I pick up a toy my babe left behind,
The tears that I cry, fall till I'm blind,
I hug my babe's toy close to my chest,
What do I do now? What's for the best?

CHAPTER 17: FIGHTING BACK

A small smile creeps across my face,
As I turn and walk away from this place,
I know one day my children will come,
I know they will know the truth.
So until that day comes, when they walk through my door,
One consolation through this hurt and this pain,
The panther will never get to hurt me again.

Chapter 18

Finally Free

I had the most wonderful opportunity to spend six months in a beautiful log cabin overlooking the Thames just outside London, to write my story. The heartache of being separated from my children still hurts deeply at times. Anyone who has been separated from their children will understand the pain of the first Christmas apart, birthdays, Mother's Day, all those special times that I had with my children are now gone for the moment. I totally believe that it is only temporary and hold on to that belief every day. Slowly, slowly I am picking up the pieces of my life. There is nothing to compare to the feeling of finally being free, nothing can compare to not looking over my shoulder any more and that terrible fear I have carried around with me for forty-five years.

Looking back I have learnt that I spent my life trying so hard to be like everyone else and to please everyone who came into my path, whatever the cost to myself, while all the time I have had this crippling pain inside for the loss of my childhood and the trauma I experienced. I have bumbled my way through life for the last forty-five years as a lost soul, and boy did I go from one disaster to another! It was not until I truly stopped and listened to my heart that day, and picked up the phone to the

CHAPTER 18: FINALLY FREE

domestic violence unit that my life started to take a turn for the better.

It is now up to me to build a happy future for myself and to have something for my children when they do come. Writing my story has been both healing and traumatic, but something I wanted to share. I have made mistakes and bad judgments throughout my life. Having written my book I can only now admit just how much the abuse I suffered especially as a child has affected my life. I feel empowered to have finally admitted just how traumatised I have been and the fear I have carried.

We all carry fear inside us, but it's when that fear becomes crippling that control of our lives starts to slip away. But we all have the power inside us to make changes in our lives, even after many years. I didn't have anyone to turn to for help, the very people I was supposed to trust and who were supposed to protect and love me, were the ones who hurt and abused me. Any abuse is horrendous, but when it is your own mother and father abusing you, the people who are supposed to set you on your way to becoming a strong, well-adjusted adult, life becomes impossible. It is incredibly difficult to talk about it because for most children who are abused, it becomes part of their lives, for many, they know no different. Many will go on being in abusive relationships, some for the rest of their lives.

Although I prayed every day for help, it was my own will to survive deep inside me that got me to take the steps I needed to leave that abusive relationship. If I had stayed any longer I would have died, either at the hands of my partner or by self-harming, that is how much despair I was feeling just before I made the call to the domestic violence unit.

I would implore anyone who is suffering abuse, if you have someone to help you, reach out to them, ask them for help. If you are alone like I was, reach deep inside yourself, you can do it, you are a precious wonderful being who only deserves the best that life has to offer. When you realise that, it is the most freeing wonderful feeling in the world.

If you know someone who is being abused, reach out to them, let them know you are there. Nobody deserves to be abused, nobody has the right to hurt another human being, and most certainly not children. The damage that is done through child abuse is immensely scarring. It is up to us as fellow human beings to stop this horrendous torture. It not only destroys childhood, gone undetected it affects the rest of your life and all those you come into contact with. Undetected it becomes a cycle of destruction and for that we must all take responsibility, we must reach out to each other, and educate our children to say 'no no no', no matter who is abusing them.

It's taken me forty-five years and a lot of heartache to have the courage to finally walk away. On my journey through life the biggest hurt apart from the abuse, is that I don't have my children. My five busy bees are angry and confused, but I pray every day that one day we will be reunited and they will understand that no matter what has happened, my love for them has never died. Until that day comes, I see a bright new future ahead, of that I am sure. If God spares me for the next forty-five years I will spend every day looking up instead of looking down. I will smile every day, and enjoy life in a way I have never had the opportunity to before.

CHAPTER 18: FINALLY FREE

Fly

Fly little bird, fly, fly, fly,
The abuse is over,
You now are strong,
So fly little bird, fly, fly, fly.
And on your journey
Promise me
Never look back
Look up with glee.
So fly little bird,
Fly, fly, fly
Now you are happy,
Now you are free.

Epilogue

So where am I now? Well, just over a year on, I am definitely turning my life around.

When I arrived in the UK, I decided it was the right time to write my story. I had tried over several years, but never succeeded. Living in such wonderful surroundings gave me the peace and the open mind to complete what I had been trying to do for so many years.

As I wrote my book, I led quite an insular life, something I felt I needed to do for a period of time. I felt I owed it to myself to take time out to reflect. It was a wonderful time filled with all kinds of emotions, some sad, some happy, and this time alone gave me the opportunity to lay the foundations I needed to start really rebuilding my life.

I would take breaks from my writing to stand outside my log cabin, smiling and embracing the beauty of the river and all the wildlife around me, watching the geese and ducks banter, play, fight and mate. I would watch a family of squirrels in amusement as they busily gathered their wares for the winter and stored them in the hollow of a big tree outside my window. I would see crows swoop down ready to pounce and take the squirrels' food, but the squirrels were far too clever and were able to outwit the crows.

EPILOGUE

Every day I felt blessed to be able to enjoy the splendour of nature all around me as it changed from winter to spring to early summer. I would smile at the simplicity of what was going on around me. I may have just written something that was very painful and traumatic, but when I stood outside and saw all the beauty, I would come back inside with wonderful pictures in my head and continue to write.

One thing I did while I was writing was join a little poetry group in the local town. I met some very lovely people and shared a wonderful evening of poetry reading. A couple of women at the group were published authors, and I mentioned I was writing a book, but had no idea how I would go about publishing it. One of the women handed me a phone number and told me that this woman would help me.

I thought I would burst with excitement at the prospect that maybe, just maybe I might get published. I sent a sample of my book to the publisher and since then I have not looked back – this wonderful woman and her team have supported, believed and encouraged me every step of the way. I never thought, through all those years of pain, I would now be sitting in the knowledge that I am a published author, something I dreamt of since I was a little girl. It was Murielle's belief in me and my story that has made this book possible.

I returned to Ireland for a time with my new loving partner Conor, a wonderful man who has shown me what it is like to be really loved. I still live in hiding from Damien, but I am happy to say that I am now in contact with my beautiful children and I know that slowly I can rebuild my relationship with them. For me that is just the most wonderful thing.

Testimonial for *Did You Hear Me Crying?*

It is an honour to write this testimonial for '*Did You Hear Me Crying?*' Cassie is a brave, strong and inspiring woman who endured and survived child abuse and domestic violence for many decades. Her story, while unique, is similar to the thousands of women affected by domestic violence who contact Women's Aid each year for help. One in five women in Ireland experience domestic violence – it can happen to any woman, in any relationship and at any age.

The insidious and pervasive nature of domestic violence, whether it is emotional, physical, sexual, or financial, is very clear from Cassie's account of her abusive marriage. The fear and anxiety that she experienced on a daily basis shows just how women become trapped in abusive relationships and how difficult it is to leave.

But women like Cassie, even at the lowest moment, resist. They face a constant battle to protect their children and themselves from their partner's relenting abuse. In very difficult circumstances, women try to make better, safer lives and give their children as much of a 'normal' existence as possible.

Sadly, as in this case, many perpetrators target children in the relationship as a way of abusing their mother. We know from our experience in Women's Aid that children are emotionally abused and used to hurt women. Often the mother and child bond is deliberately broken as a way to cause further pain and heartache for women.

This book is important. By sharing her story, Cassie helps us understand the reality of domestic violence and the journey women go through when faced with such an abuse from those closest to them.

After reading '*Did You Hear Me Crying?*' you will not ask why Cassie did not leave but rather where on earth did she find the strength and determination to survive? Her tenacity helped her rebuild her life after child abuse and 25 years of domestic violence. She shows us that it is never too late to speak up and that it is possible to move on and find love, happiness and joy in life.

Margaret Martin, Director, Women's Aid.

WOMEN'S AID
Making Women and Children Safe

About Women's Aid

Women's Aid is a leading national organisation that has been working in Ireland to stop domestic violence against women and children since 1974. In that time, Women's Aid has helped thousands of women and their children to live safer, happier lives, free from abuse.

Women's Aid runs the National Freephone Helpline 1800 341 900 (10am to 10pm, 7 days) which provides free, confidential understanding, support and information to women experiencing emotional, physical, sexual, and financial abuse by a husband, partner or boyfriend. Women's Aid also provides one to one support, advocacy and court accompaniment services and referral to local services around the country.

Women's Aid is there for women to help them make sense of what is happening, and to support them through it. The confidential and anonymous nature of the Women's Aid Helpline provides a safe, non-judgemental space for women to talk about their experiences.

One in five women in Ireland is affected by domestic violence and in 2011 Women's Aid answered over 11,000 calls from women living in fear from those closest to them – their boyfriends, partners and husbands.

Women's Aid National Freephone Helpline 1800 341 900
(10am to 10pm, 7 days a week)

For more information: www.womensaid.ie

Women's Aid is a registered charity (CHY6491).

> *"I have read so many books about death, dying and bereavement and Helen's book definitely fills the gap for those looking to make sense of dying, death and the journey through loss. Helen shares a great concept in a very readable way that we can all understand."*
>
> Carole Warren
> Interfaith Minister
> & Funeral Celebrant

This is a very personal book, which weaves Helen K Emms' own recent experience of bereavement with Spiritual-Logic insights and lessons to support the handling of death, dying and loss with a greater sense of peace.

On 21 March 2011, Helen's mother, Valerie Emms, was diagnosed with a terminal brain tumour. She died six months later. This is Helen's story. It is her mother's story and it is the story of so many other people who find out suddenly that someone they love will die within a short space of time.

Dying to Live will teach you how to use Spiritual-Logic to:

- Embrace a new, positive perspective on death and dying
- Support terminal illness through compassion, forgiveness, acceptance, patience and unconditional love
- Let go of loved ones without guilt, anger & resentment
- Celebrate personal loss with joy and love
- Live to your highest potential

60% of the Author's royalties will be donated to: Brain Tumour Research, Iain Rennie & Brain Tumour UK.

ISBN: 978-1-906954-57-4
Published: 20 September 2012
Format: Paperback
RRP: £14.99

Hurt

JULIA WEBB-HARVEY

The harrowing stories of parents whose children were sexually abused

Hurt tells the deeply moving stories of parents after they discover their child has been sexually abused. Julia Webb-Harvey beautifully narrates and facilitates parents' exploration of the truly horrible experiences –the devastation, struggles and crushing isolation - and how they set about remaking their own lives and those of their families. *Hurt* tells it like it is, tackling the social taboo of childhood sexual abuse.

"At last, thanks to Julia Webb-Harvey, a book written by experts through lived experience on the plight and courage of loving parents, who face the trauma of their child's abuse, often caused by their own partner. A must for survivors and clinicians alike."
Dr Valerie Sinason is a writer and psychoanalyst

"Hurt is an important book, which faces up to the reality of childhood sexual abuse. Hurt gives hope that families can recover, and will be a massive support to any parent/carer suffering the fallout of sexual abuse."
Denise Hubble, Clinical Services Manager, Mosac.

"Every parent should read Hurt – it is not an easy read, but it is truly amazing. The stories are haunting and will stay with me for a long time."
Karen K, parent

AWARDED BY Angels

THE TRUE STORY OF A VICTIM OF DOMESTIC VIOLENCE AND HER JOURNEY OF EMPOWERMENT

Angel Alison Ward

Today is the day you're going to die.

I've planned it all...

Those were the terrifying words Angel Alison Ward heard on the 5th July 1994, that changed her life forever.

Read Angel Alison Ward's amazing story of survival, miracles and spiritual awakening as she was shown her new path from victim-hood to empowerment.

A survivor of domestic violence, Alison is fully aware of how subtle the signs of abuse starts, now in a loving relationship and using her discovered gifts Alison is able to offer them to people from around the world.

Read her story and recognise YOU have the power to change YOUR life NOW!

Available from all good book shops and
www.amazon.co.uk and www.liveitshop.com

ISBN: 978-1-906954-44-4
Published: 21 January 2012
Format: Paperback
RRP: £14.99

live it
PUBLISHING

Dreaming of Being Published

Inspiring Authors

Sought in the fields of MBS • Psychology
Health & Healing • Personal Development
NLP • Self-Help • Business • Leadership

www.liveitpublishing.com